ENDO

Readers worldwide have been captivated and deeply impacted by weekly published articles establishing Melissa Motschenbacher as a riveting storyteller and masterful author to follow! A swelling tide of repeated reader-requests for "more—a book" led to the creation of this outstanding new daily resource devotionally designed to delight and deepen readers from all walks of life. A powerfully gifted writer and vibrant, lifestyle-practitioner of what it means to be a true, every day, everywhere "heart on fire; life on purpose," Melissa skillfully delivers stunning, humorous, creative, challenging, and practical daily devotionals that are epic and unforgettable! You are about to be inspired, laugh, grow, be challenged, and practically equipped in fresh new ways! I'm excited for YOU to experience a fire-stirring personal increase of fresh new Monumental Moments *in your life!*

~ Dwight Robertson, FORGE, Founding President & CEO, International Speaker/Author: *Plan A*, *Forged by Fire*, and *Is God Waiting for a Date with You?*

In Monumental Moments, *Melissa vulnerably shares intimate "God moments" of faith in daily pursuit of Jesus; she notes that God's presence comes as a transformative spark as one seeks a heart encounter with HIS presence. She has captured those moments for the readers in a way that encourages each to anticipate, rejoice, and reflect on personal Holy Spirit moments daily. God's presence comes uniquely in those reflective sparks of revelations we might overlook.*

~ Tom Phillips, Senior Advisor, Will Graham, Billy Graham Evangelistic Association

The personal story is like the appetizer, preparing our palate for the brief, yet poignant lesson. Then, Melissa serves the main course, the Word. It is then that you realize that today is going to be a really great day because the "Monumental Moments" we experience are sweet and deliberate whispers from God that He is always teaching us. Well done, and bon appetite!

~ Robin Sullivan, Radio Host, Evangelist, Missionary

Through my service on the Forge Board, I knew of Melissa's love for the Lord. However, when she returned from her Asbury experience, and I heard her first-hand report, it was crystal clear that Melissa had experienced truly Monumental Moments that would change her life and the lives of others dramatically, forever. We all seek that kind of a Kingdom calling and answering in our lives. Melissa has with her Monumental Moments *devotional—given us a God-breathed guide to help take our Kingdom service to new levels as we experience and recognize new Monumental Moments in our lives.* ***Thank You Melissa for allowing the Holy Spirit to reach new heights in and through you to impact our lives as we seek to become more effective Kingdom Laborers and inspire new Kingdom Laborers****. I am forever grateful for your gift and feel that all who embrace this devotional will feel the same. Praise God for* Monumental Moments *and lives changed and saved.*

~ Scott Porter, CEO, Formula Boats

There are some people you meet who carry a clear anointing to encourage and guide others in their faith—Melissa is one of them. She deeply loves the Lord and has a unique gift for helping others' faith come alive through wisdom, care, and insight. This devotional will refresh your spirit and strengthen your walk with God in powerful ways.

~ Caleb McNaughton, Lead Pastor, Highpoint Church

Monumental Moments *is a powerful devotional that invites readers to encounter God in the everyday. Through honest storytelling and Scripture-based insights, Melissa leads us to see how even life's simplest moments can become sacred. Her vulnerability, wisdom, and passion for Jesus shine through every page, encouraging us to pause, reflect, and live with eternal purpose. This isn't just a devotional—it's a call to walk closely with God and recognize His hand in all things. I highly recommend* Monumental Moments *to anyone longing to grow in faith and experience God more personally and profoundly.*

~ Amie Myers, Next Steps Pastor, Red Rocks Church, Brussels

The stories Melissa shares from her life are a true gift. They are beautiful reminders of how God speaks to us in the quiet, ordinary moments of everyday life. As we focus on these gentle nudges, we begin to recognize them as "Monumental Moments," where God reveals His unending love and forgiveness. Through this devotional, I've been inspired to reflect on my own unexpected encounters with God and have become more mindful of these moments in my daily life.

~ Karen Arangua, Owner/Operator, Chick-fil-A on Alameda Avenue, Aurora, CO

Monumental Moments *is one of the most dynamically impactful devotionals you can get your hands on today! Melissa's writing is refreshing, convicting, and inspiring—flowing right out of the pages of her own life. I have the joy of regularly working alongside Melissa, and she certainly "practices what she preaches"—always seeking to serve, humbly lifting up Jesus, and reaching those who are far from God. As you dig in, you will find yourself hungry to practice God's presence in every moment of every day!*

Don't miss your moment to encounter God and step into the adventure He has called you to!

~ Charlie Marq, International Speaker, Author, & Movement Leader, Forge (ForgeForward.org)

Amidst the quiet submission of life, one searches for the spark of God's presence, which often reveals itself in the most obscure places. This realization leads to an explosion of faith, a powerful surge that propels us forward on our spiritual journeys. Melissa's eloquent prose and heartfelt reflections serve as a compass guiding readers through the intricacies of faith, helping them to "forge" a deeper, more meaningful relationship with God. Monumental Moments, Unexpected Encounters with God . . . *the new gold-standard of kingdom-minded devotions.*

~ Nancy Eckerd, MS, RN, Author, Agape Nursing Model

If you ever meet Melissa, you'll see her running around serving, helping, and moving forward projects for the Kingdom of God, always full of joy and energy. But don't be fooled; she's sitting at Jesus' feet at all times, learning from her Master. This book is a window into those moments where He teaches her, transforms her, and loves her in so many ways. Join her in those moments, and let Jesus turn yours into Monumental Moments too!

~ Santiago Fuentes, Forge Firebrand Training Program Director & Itinerant Speaker

Monumental Moments *is a spiritual wake-up call! With captivating storytelling and biblical insight, Melissa brilliantly illuminates how God shows up in our everyday lives. She invites readers to* ***look beyond***

distractions and discover God-encounters *hiding in plain sight. This devotional will awaken you to see God's presence everywhere!*

~ Selah Hirsch, Founder and Brand Strategist, Express My Brand

Some years back I exorcized my vocabulary of the words "just" and "ordinary." Melissa is anything but "just" another writer about "ordinary" life. This devotional oozes with her contagious love for Jesus and the intimacy that is her life message. Packed with great questions, she urges her readers higher up and deeper in. In 90 days, you get to know Melissa through great stories and learn that you too can be an intimate friend of God.

~ Father Phil Eberhart, Resurrection Anglican Fellowship and Colorado Prays

Monumental Moments *is a great vehicle to bring Biblical truths and clarity to your life and your relationship with God. With real stories, reflections in Melissa's own life, Scripture references, and excellent questions, you'll gain great peace in your journey with God. Your connection with God will grow closer as you spend time in this outstanding "toolbox" on your faith journey. This book will propel you in your journey with God as it is filled with truths, clarity, inspirations, and eternal perspective He wants for each of us. You will be inspired to be hyper-receptive to what God is saying to you and how He is moving in your life. Melissa brings practical questions and very real strategic ways to be in tune with God's promises and purposes for our lives.* Monumental Moments *is written and structured in a way that reminds us of being aware and attentive to what God is calling us to do . . . even in the uncomfortable, painful moments we don't understand. I enjoyed the different sections Melissa has set up to share her real-life experiences like "Hide & Seek," "Elephant Never Forgets," and "Please Be Advised." They are very easy for real life episodes that the reader can relate to. God gives us teaching moments, and this book trains us to be aware and intentional about our time and connectedness with Him in a world of distractions. It also gives us a great sense of direction and challenges us to live to multiply His movement today.*

~ Rob Nelson, Founder and President, Heart2Hand

MONUMENTAL MOMENTS

UNEXPECTED ENCOUNTERS WITH GOD

VOLUME 1

MELISSA MOTSCHENBACHER

Monumental Moments: Unexpected Encounters* with *God

Published by Forge, 14485 East Evans Avenue, Denver, Colorado 80014

ISBN 978-1-96045-519-2 (Paperback)
ISBN 978-1-96045-520-8 (Hardback)

Visit us online at www.ForgeForward.org.

Edited by Lindsey Sims.

TABLE OF CONTENTS

FOREWORD

It's an honor to write this foreword for my friend Melissa Motschenbacher, whose life is a living testimony to what happens when we surrender ordinary moments to an extraordinary God.

I'll never forget my own Monumental Moment—a defining encounter with God that set the trajectory of my life. It didn't happen on a platform or in a church pew, but in a quiet place where I was finally honest enough to listen. When we truly open ourselves to hear His voice, He shows up—and everything changes.

Melissa lives and breathes that same truth. I've served alongside her on the mission field, and I've watched her live on mission in the everyday—whether it's ministering in the marketplace or leading her family with unwavering faith. She and her entire family are powerful examples of what it means to be Kingdom Laborers—bold, faithful, and willing to follow wherever God leads.

This devotional isn't just a collection of stories. It's an invitation to wake up each day expecting God to speak. My prayer is that, through Melissa's stories, you'll recognize your own divine appointments and say yes to the moments that can change everything.

~ Dan Cobb, Founder, Daniel Brian Advertising & MyStreme, Mission Partner, & Fellow Kingdom Laborer

DEDICATION

For those desiring to walk closely with God and find Him in everyday, ordinary moments that transform your life, this devotional is for you!

May you live to passionately pursue and proclaim Jesus. May you discover more and more of God with every story and enjoy the journey of living life with Him! Our lives can truly be one amazing parable after another, woven together into continual Monumental Moments!

I am praying for you as you journey with the Lord and have personal stories and encounters all your own. May you see Him at work every day, everywhere. Be mindful and watchful and live to seize your unexpected encounters with God!

Passionately pursuing and proclaiming Jesus with you,

— Melissa

INTRODUCTION

Every moment can be monumental and every day extraordinary with Jesus when you learn to embrace your unexpected encounters with God! He has the power to transform every part of your life and is always at work! Unfortunately, we do not always take the time to let Him.

As I continue walking with God in this faith-filled journey, I am learning the significance of seeing every ordinary moment as something extraordinary. That happens by the power and ongoing work of the Holy Spirit. He makes every moment special for all of us! They may not all be fun and easy, but they all carry the potential sparkle of a Monumental Moment!

I hunger for more of God and to pursue and proclaim Him—that, dear friend, has birthed this *Monumental Moments* devotional. The Lord has used various situations here, there, and everywhere in my day-to-day life to teach me Biblical truths in practical ways—and it has transformed my life.

Scripture is where we discover God's foundational truths about life and guidance for the moments He has given us. **Psalm 90:12** says, **"So teach us to number our days, that we may gain a heart of wisdom" (NKJV).** And **James 4:14** says, **". . . For what is your life? It is even a vapor that appears for a little time and then vanishes away" (NKJV).**

How important is it then to see every moment we have and every breath we take as a gift from God and an opportunity to know Him more? May the Lord teach us to number our days that we may gain a heart of wisdom. May we learn to seize the time we have. Every day, ordinary moments can be Monumental Moments with God.

Monumental Moments are simply God encounters. Often, they are unexpected. They are when God meets you in the middle of your daily routine, in the early morning hours, when you are reading the Bible, and in everyday situations.

May you be encouraged and inspired by this 90-day journey through modern-day parables from my life that God has used to teach me timeless truths! And may you begin to find your own Monumental Moments throughout your every day!

At the end of each devotional, you will be asked: How can you make Monumental Moments and live to multiply His movement today? This is your personal invitation to pause, pray, reflect, and consider how you can apply these Biblical truths to your life and take action!

Be vulnerable and transparent with God. Though you can read this book cover-to-cover all at once, may I suggest you take your time and linger with God, day by day? Allow Him to search your heart and lead you every step of the way.

He has Monumental Moments waiting for you!

Let's begin *your* journey to living a life of Monumental Moments with God . . .

DAY 1: PLEASE BE ADVISED

Our maximum number of checked bags per passenger were packed and overflowing to the point they could barely zip shut. Everything was in order, and all the to-dos were checked off the list to start our long-awaited vacation. My husband and I were ready to leave for the airport with my parents within the hour for our flight.

Drinking our morning coffee and orange juice together at the hotel restaurant, we were suddenly made aware of an email from the airline that hit my mom's inbox first. It was a dreaded "Please Be Advised" notification. Good news, the flight was on time—enter a unison sigh of relief! Yay, the vacation is still scheduled as planned! At least we would be on island time soon enough!

So, what was the problem? The airline wanted the passengers to be advised there was an issue with the Wi-Fi. They wanted to notify everyone the Wi-Fi was out of service for the upcoming 8-hour, international flight! Did I just hear you gasp with me? What on earth does someone do for 8 hours without Wi-Fi anymore—especially on a long flight, belted into a small seat with virtually nothing to do?

I had to give myself a slight pep talk to overcome the kink in my agenda for the day. I had plans to catch up on email and finish a few ministry projects before reaching the islands and being unplugged for a bit.

Well, there is a trend when things like this happen in my world. God uses everything like this as a teaching moment for me. They become Monumental Moments in my life. I knew God was about to sit me down for another one-on-one coaching session. It was time to look at the priorities in my life. I knew the Lord was putting His finger on something yet again.

I became keenly aware I was more internally consumed with not having Wi-Fi and being disconnected from the internet and the world than I have been from being disconnected with the Almighty God. How can I spend more time being worried about not having a man-made lifeline to the world than being worried about disconnection with the Creator and lover of my soul?

Suddenly, my heart broke. It broke for: time wasted and consumed with trivial distractions; personal daily agendas that have left God stood-up again without me showing up; me hearing but not intently listening to His voice; and me even disobeying Him.

Have you ever been there? Maybe, it's just me. I am embarrassed to say I have put more intentionality and concern toward the importance of being connected to the internet over being connected to my Father. There are times I am more consumed with being disconnected from the world, people, and things than to my precious Heavenly Father.

I am thankful the Lord doesn't leave us where we are, but He challenges us, teaches us, corrects us, and equips us for this journey of life! Thank the Lord for the truth of the Word of God that gives us a firm foundation to live by.

Psalm 139:23-24 says, "**Search me, O God, and know my heart! Try me and know my thoughts! And see if there be any grievous way in me and lead me in the way everlasting!**"

Are you concerned that you may be disconnected with God? He is waiting to meet with you at this very moment! Will you allow God to search your heart today and see if there is anything within you that grieves His heart? Will you draw close to Him? He loves you enough to grow you more and more into His image!

How can you make Monumental Moments and live to multiply His movement today?

DAY 2: NO MORE HIDE AND SEEK

Have you ever watched a child have the time of their life running, giggling, and trying to find the next great hiding spot as they play the classic game Hide and Seek? It's a game filled with a roller coaster of emotions. There is excitement, joy, anticipation, fun, and even anxiety. While everyone runs to find the best location to hide, the person that will be on the adventure trying to find everyone closes their eyes and begins to count out loud to 100. Sometimes, it's as simple as them saying, "One, two, skip a few, one hundred!" Then they yell and warn everyone, "Ready or not, here I come!" They take off running to try and quickly discover anyone that is hiding. The others wait and wait, trying to refrain from any movement that would cause noise and simultaneously control their heavy breathing all while hoping they will not get discovered. In their mind, the longer they are undetected the better!

It's all fun and games and lighthearted, until one day you wake up and realize you are in the middle of a game of Hide and Seek, but this time with God.

In my quiet time alone with God recently I asked Him, "What is it that you want me to know Lord?" I try to be very careful declaring God says something or saying, "Thus sayeth the Lord." This particular night, I knew the Lord dropped something profound in my heart. I was fully aware the Lord was impressing something deep within my spirit. I felt as though He was revealing, "I am tired of playing Hide and Seek."

I know God never tires or grows weary, but it was His way of getting my attention and speaking straight to my heart. In my childish response, I pushed back and declared, "Lord, Hide and Seek is for two-year-olds." I knew the Lord had more to say and was asking me a very direct question: "Melissa, when was the first game of Hide and Seek?" Instantly, the Lord brought the Garden of Eden to mind when Adam and Eve hid from God after they sinned.

Genesis 3:6-10 recounts the moment:

> **So when the woman saw that the tree was good for food, that it was pleasant to the eyes, and a tree desirable to make one wise, she took of its fruit and ate. She also gave to her husband with her, and he ate. Then the eyes of both of them were opened, and they knew that they were naked; and they sewed fig leaves together and made themselves coverings. And they heard the sound of the Lord God walking in the garden in the cool of the day, and Adam and his wife hid themselves from the presence of the Lord God among the trees of the garden. Then the Lord God called to Adam and said to him, "Where are you?" So he said, "I heard Your voice in the garden, and I was afraid because I was naked; and I hid myself" (NKJV).**

After I read this Scripture again, I knew the Lord wanted me to stop playing games with Him and to stop hiding. I had a heavy conviction. It can be so easy to be chasing after God one minute and hiding from Him the next.

I had been disobeying God and running from Him and the plans and call He had on my life. I can sin through delay, and I can sin out of willful defiance. Sin in any form keeps us hiding from God.

The Lord brings clarity and conviction, but the enemy brings confusion and condemnation. Conviction draws our heart back to the Father, while condemnation can keep us hiding from the Father.

I believe mankind, me included, has been playing Hide and Seek with God since the fall of man—just one and two chapters after we read about the creation of man. We run to God, walk with Him, commune with Him, love Him, and then suddenly lay it all aside to chase the next best sparkly or new thing in the moment. We run from God and leave Him waiting. We leave Him asking, "Where are you?" He is faithful and steadfast. We are the ones running and hiding from Him. Ultimately, He knows where we are. He is God. He is waiting for us to stop running and hiding.

Are you in the middle of a game of Hide and Seek with God? Pause and let Him search your heart.

Kingdom Laborers . . . it's time we stop playing games with God. No more Hide and Seek. Let's be found constantly walking with Him step by step and not running from Him.

What secret are you hiding from God? Reveal it, and let it be exposed before Him. He loves you!

How can you make Monumental Moments and live to multiply His movement today?

DAY 3: BROKEN BUTTERFLIES

Kodak moments and highlight reels have a special way of taking us down memory lane.

I don't know what it was that triggered this memory, but I was reminded of a treasured moment recently. It was a precious season of life. I had only been a mother for a couple of years at the time, so I was still trying to figure out this new title and life as a mom. Doing my best to get my daughter out of the house and on adventures, we headed to the park for a playdate.

After a few hours at the park and a chicken nugget happy meal with fries in the classic, red and yellow cardboard box, it was time for a little shopping in our historic downtown district. We walked the street together window shopping until we came to the Christian bookstore.

Being a new believer, I couldn't resist going into the store. The Bibles, commentaries, Bible studies, and Scriptures stamped on all sorts of merchandise were calling my name. I decided to wheel the little stroller in and browse the aisles for a while.

Getting quickly lost in time and in the middle of a Bible study index, I heard, "Look, Mommy," *(pronounced: "Yook, Mommy").* A shatter then immediately got my attention. The tiny hands from my umbrella stroller beneath me had decided to do some shopping as well.

My young daughter was drawn to a colorful, ceramic butterfly steppingstone that had Scripture engraved around the edging. Suddenly, the store owner came running our way. I bent down to start picking up the pieces, while apologizing religiously. The store owner said, "Don't worry, honey. I will put all the pieces in a bag for you when you check out. Someone has to pay for this, and it can't be our store."

Frustrated and yelling at my daughter, I gathered our broken pieces and immediately walked to the counter to check out. Embarrassed and heartbroken, we exited the store together with a new, broken butterfly. I kept wondering how on earth I would explain this to my husband, since we were knee-deep in credit card debt at the time, and this was certainly not in the budget.

That broken butterfly quickly became a cherished piece of art in our flower garden and would last for many years to come. I kept it as a reminder that "Someone has to pay for this!" Every single time I saw the glued, broken steppingstone, I couldn't help but thank God that He sent His only Son, Jesus Christ, to pay the price for my sins, my family's sins, the world's sins, and our broken lives.

Someone had to pay the price for sin and brokenness. The Good News is, Jesus paid the price. He did that for you, for me, and all of mankind. He paid it all when He died on the cross, was buried, and resurrected.

Do you have broken pieces of your life that you have not allowed God to mend? Have you offered your life completely to the One who can restore you fully? Look to Jesus Christ, the One who paid the price for your sin and brokenness. The cost was weighty, but He knew *YOU* were worth it!

This is a valuable pause point to look at the Bible and what it says about the price that was paid for you and me—specifically, as outlined throughout the Romans Road.

- **"For all have sinned and fall short of the glory of God." Romans 3:23**

- **"For the wages of sin is death, but the free gift of God is eternal life in Christ Jesus our Lord." Romans 6:23**

- **"But God shows His love for us in that while we were still sinners, Christ died for us." Romans 5:8**

- **"Because, if you confess with your mouth that Jesus is Lord and believe in your heart that God raised Him from the dead, you will be saved. For with the heart one believes and is justified, and with the mouth one confesses and is saved." Romans 10:9-10**

- **"For 'everyone who calls on the name of the Lord will be saved.'" Romans 10:13**

Will you take a moment and thank God for paying the ultimate price when He died on the cross for your sins—making a way for you to be whole again? He is the only One that can put back together the brokenness we carry.

Is there someone around you broken and hurting that needs to hear about Jesus as their Savior? Will you share your testimony of the broken butterflies in your life that Jesus has restored?

How can you make Monumental Moments and live to multiply His movement today?

DAY 4: AN ELEPHANT NEVER FORGETS

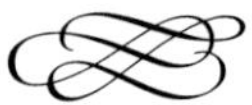

We finally made it!

We dreamed, saved, planned, prepared, cashed in hotel points, used airline miles, and all the perks possible to travel thousands of miles to the other side of the world. It was no small undertaking.

It sounds glamorous, but there was a cost!

We took the cheap seats! You know, the ones at the back of the plane by the bathrooms. We forfeited direct flights, chose multiple stops and long layovers, and used multiple airline carriers and partners to travel as cheaply as possible.

As my husband says, "You pay for it one way or another!" He was right. We had well over 30 hours of travel in each direction.

But we made it to Phuket, Thailand. It was beautiful. The people, the culture, the food, and the scenery were all amazing. It was an incredible experience.

One night, after a long day of rotating between the infinity pool and playing in the ocean, we took time to slow down even more, to take in the mesmerizing beauty of the spectacular sunset.

With just a few clouds suspended in the pale blue sky, giving the illusion of fluffy cotton candy, our hearts were captivated. The sun refused to linger and quickly disappeared behind the depths of the ocean blue.

We sat speechless, hand in hand, admiring God's matchless masterpiece.

I must admit, now that I am getting older, my eyes aren't as sharp as they once were. Taking time to readjust to the increasingly darker sky, I continued to scan the horizon, the ocean, and the seashore, while thanking God for another wonderful day and experience.

As I looked off into the distance, watching the gentle waves continually massage the sandy seashore, I was surprised. I broke the silence, pointed toward the south, and told my husband, "Look how close that boat is to the shore."

I was shocked. This large, faint blob (according to my tired eyes) was at the water's edge and appeared to have run aground, yet it was moving slowly in our direction.

We both sat and stared. To my surprise, my husband said, "Melissa, that is not a boat. That's an elephant."

What! An elephant?

I knew we were in Thailand, but an elephant taking a stroll on the beach was another level.

My husband went on to reassure me that an elephant was headed in our direction. We both jumped up simultaneously and started running—not from the elephant, but to it!

Scott was right. There was an elephant on the beach in Phuket, Thailand.

My older eyes, though tired from a full, sun-kissed day and salty seawater exposure, began to see it plain as day. Suddenly, we were face to face with an elephant!

A local man was simply out riding his elephant, as casually as you or I would walk our dog on the beach. We took a moment to greet them both and fed the elephant a few palm tree leaves. It was a sight to behold. We really haven't stopped talking about the experience.

I have to laugh when I think about the initial image. I thought I saw a boat. As you know, there is a big difference between a boat and an elephant!

With a little help, the Lord quickly brought the image into perspective for me. God is good at doing that for all of us! He sent His Son, Jesus Christ, that we could see and experience the fullness of His eternal love for us. He desires to have living encounters with us! He sends His Holy Spirit to continue to guide, teach, correct, reveal, heal, and encourage us, moment by moment, no matter where we are.

This experience in Thailand made me think of the blind man in **Mark 8:22-25**:

> **They came to Bethsaida, and some people brought a blind man and begged Jesus to touch him. He took the blind man by the hand and led him outside the village. When He had spit on the man's eyes and put His hands on him, Jesus asked, 'Do you see anything?' He looked up and said, 'I see people; they look like trees walking around.' Once more Jesus put His hands on the man's eyes. Then his eyes were opened, his sight was restored, and he saw everything clearly (NIV).**

Jesus changes everything. He led the man, step by step, into full sight. The man went from being blind, to seeing walking trees, to seeing everything clearly.

God helped me go from seeing an illusion of a boat to seeing an actual live elephant in front of us. God heals physically and spiritually.

Have you positioned yourself next to Jesus and begged Him for full clarity? Have you allowed Him to lead you, touch your heart, question you, and heal you? Has He helped you to see things differently?

Take a moment now and ask God to open your spiritual eyes that you would see everything clearly!

There is an old saying, "An elephant never forgets." May that be our anthem as children of God. May we never forget Christ and all that He has done for us and continues to do to bring clarity and eternal perspective.

How can you make Monumental Moments and live to multiply His movement today?

DAY 5: WARNING—ROAD WORK AHEAD

We were back in our home state of Michigan recently to spend time with family—checking on some and celebrating birthdays with others. We drove from one side of the state to the other. Not much has changed in the beautiful state since we moved.

It has been said, "There are two seasons in Michigan: winter, and construction." You may laugh at that saying, but if you have driven through Michigan in the summer, you understand the pain. It seemed to be the case yet again this summer. There was a world of bright orange scattered amidst the confines of the gorgeous Great Lakes!

There were construction signs everywhere. Signs like: Caution, Reduced Speed Ahead, Road Closure Ahead, Detour, Construction Zone, Road Work Ahead, Road Construction Next 8 Miles, Speed Fines Doubled in Construction Zones and on and on. I am sure you are familiar with signs like these.

The roads—interstates, back roads, dirt roads, and paved roads were filled with orange warning signs, barricades, barrels, construction cones, construction workers, large machinery and newly formed rumble strips. You learn to calculate accordingly and add on an extra few minutes or *hour* to your commute!

The construction made me think of what I read on Ruth Bell Graham's gravestone once, "End of Construction—Thank you for your patience."

Sitting in traffic at a complete standstill and growing increasingly frustrated, I had time to ask myself a few pointed questions. Is my life open to the work of the Holy Spirit? As I travel on life's road that God has me on, am I open to His work and dealings? I know there have been times I have tried to detour on my own. There have been times I have wanted to bypass God's construction work. We can get that way with the Lord at times. We can take our own detours to try and bypass the work of God just as quickly as we make our own detours to bypass road construction.

Philippians 1:6 says, **"I am sure of this, that He who started a good work in you will carry it on to completion until the day of Christ Jesus" (CSB).**

Philippians 2:12-13 says,

> **Therefore, my dear friends, just as you have always obeyed, so now, not only in my presence but even more in my absence, work out your own salvation with fear and trembling. For it is God who is working in you both to will and to work according to His good purpose (CSB).**

Ephesians 3:20-21 reminds us,

> **Now to Him who is able to do far more abundantly than all that we ask or think, according to the power at work within us, to Him be glory in the church and in Christ Jesus throughout all generations, forever and ever. Amen.**

When is the last time you have welcomed or even asked for God's construction work in your life? I understand it can be challenging, slow, and even painful at times, but it's transforming!

Will you take time now to ask God to reveal areas that need work in your life? Ask Him to expose the cracks and potholes and to give you the wisdom, strength, and power of the Holy Spirit to continue walking in the work He began in you. You can't do this on your own! You need the Holy Spirit! Watch for warning and caution signs from God and proceed accordingly! Don't make your own detours!

How can you make Monumental Moments and live to multiply His movement today?

DAY 6: DO YOU GO TO CHURCH?

My husband and I got the privilege to travel with my parents to Belize for a week of sailing. Let me tell you, it was soggy and salty, but fun nonetheless! We were out at sea in the middle of a tropical storm, though we didn't realize it at the time. Rain, rain, and more rain. EIGHTEEN inches of measured rain to be exact!

At one point our designated meteorologist, my mother, pulled up the sailing weather app to consider our sail plan for the day as we sat rocking by the waves while tied to a mooring ball. The weather was crazy! For but a moment, we were sitting dead center in the middle of the tropical storm—the eye of the storm. There were somewhat calm seas under our boat, but rain, weather, winds, and grey clouds were at every turn. As far as the eye could see, for 360 degrees, it was dark and notably stormy.

We talked, read, played cards and bingo, and stared off into the distance. At one point my husband said, "What are you thinking about?"

"Lilliana," I replied. Despite the storm brewing around us, I could not stop thinking about a young woman we met recently named Lilliana.

Before we sailed out to sea, we went to grab lunch at a local Belizean restaurant. It was "UnBelizeable," as they say in Belize! Not because of the food, but because of what happened at the lunch table! It wasn't just another meal at a restaurant. It was a divine appointment. The Lord prompted me to begin conversation with our waitress. I asked her name, complimented the beautiful restaurant, and asked her how long she had been working there. Her name was Lilliana, and she was the sweetest young woman. The conversation carried on, and then I knew the Lord was asking me to tell her about Jesus!

It may sound funny, but often when I feel led to share Christ with someone without knowing their story, at some point, I will ask the question, "So, do you go to church?" From there, it helps me know which way to direct the conversation. For Lilliana, the answer was, "No."

The Lord directed our conversation. After asking, "Why," it led me to explain, "I understand. I have been there too." I told Lilliana, "I have been where you are, but Jesus changed everything for me." I explained, He could do that for her too! After sharing, asking, and listening to Lilliana, I invited her to accept Jesus as her Lord and Savior. Lilliana said no one has ever told her about Jesus and what He did for her. I pulled up a seat, invited her to sit down, and offered her an invitation to receive Christ. She said she was ready to receive Jesus as her Lord and Savior! I grabbed her hands and prayed with Lilliana to receive Jesus Christ. With tears and thanksgiving, we celebrated that moment. Lilliana messaged me the next day and said, "I feel different today. I have so much joy in my heart."

What a moment to celebrate!

Matthew 5:13-16 says,

You are the salt of the earth; but if the salt loses its flavor, how shall it be seasoned? It is then good for nothing but to be thrown out and trampled underfoot by men. You are the light of the world. A city that is set on a hill cannot be hidden. Nor do they light a lamp and

> **put it under a basket, but on a lampstand, and it gives light to all who are in the house. Let your light so shine before men, that they may see your good works and glorify your Father in heaven (NKJV).**

In this Scripture, salt is used to describe how we can infuse and flavor the world with the Good News of Jesus, seasoning everyone we encounter with His love. So, let's remain salty!

From sailing the salty seas, to being the salt of the earth, we have to remain salty! There is a term used in sailing, "salty sailor"—it simply means a sailor who has been toughened by experience! A sailor has a job to work the boat! We have a job to work the harvest fields—land and sea, and everywhere the Lord takes us.

Let's be salty sailors, seasoned and experienced when it comes to navigating the seas of conversation!

How can you start a conversation with someone and tell them about your Savior, Jesus Christ? Will you take it further still and go from sharing about Him to inviting them to receive Him as their personal Lord and Savior?

How can you make Monumental Moments and live to multiply His movement today?

DAY 7: LICENSE, REGISTRATION, & PROOF OF INSURANCE

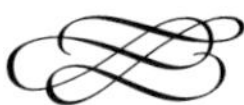

Often, as one year comes to a close and a new year rolls around, I sit before the Lord in prayer asking Him for guidance, wisdom, a word, a scripture, direction, and a focus for the year ahead. This year's word was a bit different. I first felt the Lord drop *intimacy* in my heart. I was to focus on intimacy with Him more than ever before.

Last year was a powerful year drawing closer to the Lord after an incredible encounter at the Asbury Revival, but as always there is still more of God to discover. My heart beats and longs to be intimately close with the Father, but I know He longs for me even more. As a parent, I can relate to the excitement of spending precious time with my child.

Beginning to prepare for intentional ways to deepen my journey and time with Him, to my surprise, another word dropped in my heart. This time, it was the word *discipline*. I wrote *intimacy* at the top, center of the first page of my notebook and *discipline* directly under it. Suddenly, a third word was revealed—an acronym. As I stared at the words *intimacy* and *discipline,* I realized there was an acronym of *ID*.

The Lord began to show me something special. I knew it would take continued discipline to remain in a state of intimacy with the

Lord, and as a byproduct it would bring forth the fullness on my identity in Christ. Discipline to stay close with Him will continue to remind me of my identity in Him. Instead of the world telling me who I am and what I am not, discipline to remain in an intimate walk with God will continually reveal my true identity. It will reveal who He says I am: a child of the Most-High God, fiercely loved, a friend of His, and fearfully and wonderfully made. It will allow me to see my ID fully and completely rooted in Him. It helps me navigate life, decisions, relationships, choices, and perspectives when I know where my identity lies—in Him. It gives me Heavenly authority that sometimes I forget I have.

We all have ID's we use like a driver's license, social security number, passport, military card, loyalty card, student card, reward's card, and even more adventurous items like a scuba diving certification or sailing credential card! IDs are an important part of our lives. In fact, we can't legally drive a car or travel on a plane without them.

So, do I understand the fullness of my ID in Christ? Have I placed more value on other worldly IDs? It's time I give myself a continual reminder of who I am in Christ as I stay disciplined and focused on intimacy with Him.

Let's remember these truths:

- **"Therefore, if anyone is in Christ, he is a new creation. The old has passed away; behold, the new has come." 2 Corinthians 5:17**

- **"'In Him we live and move and have our being;' as even some of your own poets have said, 'for we are indeed His offspring.'" Acts 17:28**

- **"For in Christ Jesus you are all sons of God, through faith." Galatians 3:26**

- **"For those whom He foreknew He also predestined to be conformed to the image of His Son, in order that He might be the firstborn among many brothers." Romans 8:29**

- **"So God created man in His own image, in the image of God He created him; male and female He created them." Genesis 1:27, NKJV**

- **"I praise you, for I am fearfully and wonderfully made. Wonderful are Your works; my soul knows it very well." Psalm 139:14**

- **"But to all who did receive Him, who believed in His name, He gave the right to become children of God." John 1:12**

- **"The Lord appeared to him from far away. I have loved you with an everlasting love; therefore, I have continued my faithfulness to you." Jeremiah 31:3**

- **"And the Scripture was fulfilled that says, Abraham believed God, and it was counted to him as righteousness —and he was called a friend of God." James 2:23**

What's the most important ID you carry? Or, as the world says, "What's in your wallet?" Is your ID in Christ the most important ID you have?

How can you make Monumental Moments and live to multiply His movement today?

DAY 8: SUPER-SIZE ME

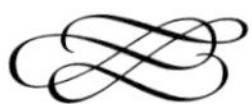

Life is never boring traveling with my husband! NEVER. In fact, I am at the point I keep a travel journal for the crazy adventures we share together. Today, I am going to let you in on one of the many little escapades that made my travel journal recently. We headed to the Nashville airport to catch a flight to Michigan. Being around the dinner hour, my husband made his way to one of the restaurants for a Mediterranean dinner. We ordered our food and stepped over to the side to stand in line as they prepared the takeout meals.

My husband also ordered a soda, which he normally doesn't do. We stood in line, waited, and curved around the stanchions patiently while we debriefed the day's events and planned for the trip to Michigan. As we made it closer to the server behind the glass window to customize our plates, my husband sat his drink on the counter and began pointing to the various vegetables and toppings he wanted with his chicken shawarma and rice. We quickly grabbed our Styrofoam containers and headed to find an empty table in the busy airport food court. We sat down, thanked God, prayed for our meal, and began to open our plates to enjoy a quick dinner before our upcoming flight.

But first . . . my husband grabbed the cup on the table and took a long sip. Suddenly, I heard obsessive slurping—the kind of slurping that happens at the bottom of an incredible milkshake until that very last drop is gone. Or the kind of slurping that happens at the bottom of an ice-filled fountain drink on a hot summer day.

That's odd, I thought to myself, he just purchased that large soda. Then, came a look of confusion and, beyond that, pure shock on his face. He quickly realized this was not his drink in his hand, nor his straw in his mouth, but a random empty cup that was left on the food court table from a stranger! My husband had left his full glass of soda on the counter when he was customizing his order. Thirsty and in a hurry, he sucked the already empty cup dry. Slurping all the way to the end, until there was not a drop left, he unapologetically made sure everyone around him heard it as if he were finishing the greatest smoothie, shake, or Slurpee on the planet!

Reliving the moment play-by-play, over and over in my head allowed God to teach me something. I felt as though I was to consider the last time I have been desperate and thirsty for more of God—knowing He has a cup that never runs dry! Does my spiritual cup run over, or am I parched and desperately grasping for straws? Have you ever found yourself empty and not running to God for endless refills? He has living water that will allow us to never thirst again!

His Word says this:

- **"On the last day of the feast, the great day, Jesus stood up and cried out, 'If anyone thirsts, let him come to Me and drink. Whoever believes in Me, as the Scripture has said, "out of his heart will flow rivers of living water."' Now this He said about the Spirit, whom those who believed in Him were to receive, for as yet the Spirit had not been given, because Jesus was not yet glorified." John 7:37-39**

- **"And the Lord will guide you continually and satisfy your desire in scorched places and make your bones**

strong; and you shall be like a watered garden, like a spring of water, whose waters do not fail." Isaiah 58:11

- **"Jesus answered her, 'If you knew the gift of God, and who it is that is saying to you, "Give Me a drink," you would have asked Him, and He would have given you living water.'" John 4:10**

- **"As the deer pants for streams of water, so my soul pants for You, O God. My soul thirsts for God, for the living God. When can I go and meet with God? My tears have been my food day and night, while men say to me all day long, 'Where is your God?'" Psalm 42:1, NIV**

- **"You prepare a table before me in the presence of my enemies; You anoint my head with oil; my cup overflows." Psalm 23:5**

Don't rely on others or be left holding an empty cup. God can give you a supersized portion of living water with bottomless refills! What are you waiting for? Take your cup back again today for more of God! What is it that you need from Him today?

How can you make Monumental Moments and live to multiply His movement today?

DAY 9: STRETCH MARKS

Many would agree, there really isn't anything glamorous about stretch marks. Often, people do their best to cover them up or get them medically removed.

Yet hidden very well, everyone in my family has them. Some stretch marks were born almost overnight as quickly as the kids grew tall—inch by inch. Others appeared with the slow burn of muscle development. And others still were birthed out of a long, nine-month pregnancy journey. Regardless, they all have one thing in common—pain and stretching. No matter the root cause, it was growth that birthed the stretch marks into existence.

Seeing physical stretch marks on my body makes me wonder whether I have spiritual growing pains and stretch marks as well! Am I doing my best to fight and resist them? Has my faith been tested and stretched? Is there a noticeable difference that I can visualize? Can others notice a difference in me? These are all fair and valid questions to ask.

How about you? Has the Lord stretched you recently, pushing you to grow in areas that have made you taller and stronger? Are you physically birthing God-sized dreams into existence with the help of the Lord? If not, it may be time to ask Him to continue to grow your faith!

The Bible reminds us of great truths regarding growth!

- **"Consider it a sheer gift, friends, when tests and challenges come at you from all sides. You know that under pressure, your faith-life is forced into the open and shows its true colors. So don't try to get out of anything prematurely. Let it do its work, so you become mature and well-developed, not deficient in any way." James 1:2-4, MSG**

- **"Not only that, but we rejoice in our sufferings, knowing that suffering produces endurance, and endurance produces character, and character produces hope, and hope does not put us to shame, because God's love has been poured into our hearts through the Holy Spirit who has been given to us. For while we were still weak, at the right time Christ died for the ungodly." Romans 5:3-6**

In what areas can you ask God to increase your faith so you can continue to see tangible growth in your walk with Him? Are you bearing fruit?

I am cheering for you and praying with you! Let's ask God to stretch us—that we may continue to grow more and more into His image.

How can you make Monumental Moments and live to multiply His movement today?

DAY 10: THE CHOSEN RESUME

I watch my husband, who has a career in sales, work harder and harder to button up orders at the end of every quarter. With ever-growing demands, quotas are always increasing. It often feels like sales come down to the wire. He has learned to work hard and trust God in the process.

Recently as he worked diligently to close many lingering sales opportunities, he also sifted through piles of résumés sitting on his desk to try and hire for open positions within his territory.

One by one, he read the highly edited marketing documents that showcased the many accomplishments of talented candidates from around the country. From a simple piece of paper representing all the highlights of a person's career, he chose the top candidates to advance to an initial phone screening.

I couldn't help but walk by his desk seeing the stack of resumes and think to myself, *God, I am so thankful you chose me for your Kingdom work despite my lowly and horrific life resume.* As we know, resumes highlight all of our accolades for others to see. I don't have anything flashy to bring to the table.

What does God see? Instead of a list of God-honoring

achievements and accomplishments that I could bring before the King, I only had a resume defaming the name of the Lord.

John 15:16 says, "**You did not choose Me, but I chose you and appointed you that you should go and bear fruit, and that your fruit should remain, that whatever you ask the Father in My name He may give you" (NKJV).**

No matter your resume and no matter where you are on your journey with God, know this—He chose you. He has appointed you that you should *go* and *bear fruit—fruit that should remain!*

Oh, how amazing to know we have been chosen! We are His chosen ones to work for His Kingdom. There is no competition! You are not sitting in the midst of a pile of Kingdom résumés waiting to be called upon. You *are* the chosen one!

Run the race set before you. Own it. Work the harvest fields for the greatest employer in the world! Build His Kingdom by advancing His mission and spreading His name and fame! You've got this because He has you!

What harvest fields might God be calling you to this year? Where is He asking you to bear fruit?

How can you make Monumental Moments and live to multiply His movement today?

DAY 11: PERFECT HARMONY

Here's another honest, real-life mess-up that was crowned with the redeeming work of the Holy Spirit. We sold our home recently to downsize. We have been waiting, seeking, praying, and asking God to guide our next steps. It's been a process.

We found a modest ranch that caught our eye but didn't necessarily capture our hearts initially. We prayed, asked for God's wisdom and clarity, read His Word trusting it would speak to us, and we yielded our plans to His. Our realtor continued to ask, "What exactly are you looking for?" We couldn't put our finger on it other than to use the word, "Sanctuary."

As I prayed about this home that happened to originally be built for a wounded soldier, I asked the Lord if it would be a good fit for us. I felt as though the Lord put a simple question in my heart . . . "Are you not a wounded soldier?"

In no way do I want to diminish the sacrifice of those willing to give their lives for our freedom. I am so thankful for their extravagant sacrifice. I do not believe this was a question referring to my physical state, but I knew the Lord was referring to my soul and spiritual journey as His Christian soldier. I thought, *Yes, Lord,* I am a wounded soldier in Your Kingdom.

Instantly, I knew, that I knew, that I knew, the Lord was saying, "This home is a 'Sanctuary for Soldiers!'" That's all we needed to move forward. The home needed work and would be a project before we could move in. However, that week we made an offer. Our offer was rejected. So, we continued in our house hunting adventures while continually keeping an eye on this home. Weeks later, we still couldn't shake it. It was the topic of many conversations and the destination of many late-night car rides.

After continual prayers and further promptings from the Holy Spirit, Scott and I decided to make another offer. We put a plan in place, got pre-approved, and called our realtor to get a second offer in motion. Sounds great, right? It was more complicated than that. It came with lengthy and even heated arguments as we negotiated an offer—not with the buyer but amongst ourselves. Scott wanted to honor the buyer and honor the nudging of the Holy Spirit to do what we needed to do to purchase this home. I wanted to honor God and be good stewards of the resources He has put in our care and try to stretch every dollar. We both were right but went about it entirely wrong. Regardless, we proceeded amid tension.

The next day, our offer was presented to the buyer. Moments later, we received a call from our realtor to explain there was already another offer on the table, and it was higher than ours. All we could do was wait to see how it played out before the contract was due to expire at 4 p.m.

But, at 1 p.m., I felt burdened deep within my soul to hit my knees and pray. While praying, I quickly realized it wasn't about praying for the home, but rather the current state of our marriage and our hearts. Scott and I were moving forward in something and were not unified as a married couple. The Holy Spirit corrected me instantly. I knew the Holy Spirit was revealing to me Scott and I were not walking in unity and reminding me where there is unity, He commands a blessing. I wept. I repented. I jumped up. I ran to Scott. I apologized. I asked for forgiveness. I explained what the Lord taught me, and we prayed together, repented together, and read **Psalm 133:1-3** together which says:

> **Behold, how good and pleasant it is when brothers dwell in unity! It is like the precious oil on the head, running down on the beard, on the beard of Aaron, running down on the collar of his robes! It is like the dew of Hermon, which falls on the mountains of Zion! For there the LORD has commanded the blessing, life forevermore.**

4 p.m. came and went, and our offer expired. At 4:50 p.m., the phone rang. The call was from our realtor. He said, "Well. . . it's hard to explain this. You know the other offer was higher, but the buyer wants to work with you! There may be a small counteroffer coming that we should receive within 15 minutes. Moments later we were under contract on a home that will be a "Sanctuary for Kingdom soldiers!"

Brothers and sisters . . . live to dwell in unity. It's like the precious oil running down heads, beards, collars, and robes . . . for there the LORD has commanded the blessing, life forevermore!

Will you pray and ask the Lord to reveal where you may be lacking unity? Then, repent, ask for forgiveness, and be expectant for God to move!

How can you make Monumental Moments and live to multiply His movement today?

DAY 12: MORE THAN A TURKEY TROT

"Well, you got yourself in another boondoggle," is exactly what my father-in-law would have said if he were there. Truthfully, he would have been right.

I exited the taxi, entered the Denver International Airport, briskly walked to security, and then down the escalator to the train to head to my terminal. At least that was the plan. Instead, I was held up in the train for a bit—literally. It's comical now, but it wasn't at the moment. I rushed onto the airport train right behind my husband just before the doors closed—squeezing into the last available space possible.

The train took off quickly as everyone was fighting for their balance and personal space! It must have looked like a scene from a movie. But unfortunately, it was all too real. Suddenly, I realized I was stuck. My long hair was tangled and closed in the train door, and I couldn't move until the doors reopened at the next stop.

My husband seized the moment and took the opportunity to take a photo and laugh simultaneously. I'm sure it looked funny to everyone on the train! I was stuck dead in my tracks, and not by choice! I couldn't move if I wanted to.

As I stood still until the next train stop, I had a couple of moments to think. I realized how quickly it all transpired. It was a great visual representation of how easy it is to get tangled physically and even spiritually.

Have you ever found yourself in a situation you could have prevented? In hindsight, we may realize we could have made better choices, prepared more, or even taken precautionary measures along the way.

Hebrews 12:1-3 says,

> **Therefore, since we are surrounded by such a great cloud of witnesses, let us throw off everything that hinders and the sin that so easily entangles. And let us run with perseverance the race marked out for us, fixing our eyes on Jesus, the pioneer and perfecter of faith. For the joy set before Him He endured the cross, scorning its shame, and sat down at the right hand of the throne of God. Consider Him who endured such opposition from sinners, so that you will not grow weary and lose heart (NIV).**

There was no way I was running in this moment. I was entangled. I had to use this as another teaching moment and ask, "What is hindering or entangling me spiritually? What can I do to better run my race for God with perseverance as I fix my eyes on Jesus?"

How about you? This is more than a Turkey Trot or Christmas 5k we are running! We are all running a race that leads to eternity. We must fix our eyes on Jesus, run the race marked out for us, and throw off everything that is hindering and entangling us. Are you tangled in a mess that needs God's intervention? Have you called out to Him?

Let's not wait until we are stuck literally. Listen to the Holy Spirit in your life and His convictions and follow His lead!

How can you make Monumental Moments and live to multiply His movement today?

DAY 13: DO YOU KNOW THE MUFFIN MAN?

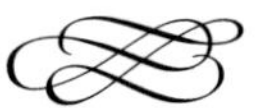

There is a traditional nursery rhyme called, *The Muffin Man.* You may have heard it a time or two. It recites like this, "Do you know the muffin man, the muffin man, the muffin man? Do you know the muffin man, who lives on Drury Lane?" It continues with a response, "Yes, I know the muffin man, the muffin man, the muffin man. Yes, I know the muffin man, who lives on Drury Lane." And on and on it goes on repeat!

Well . . . I haven't met the muffin man who lives on Drury Lane, but I did unexpectedly meet the Bible man who may buy and sell on Drury Lane!

I went out shopping for presents one cold, snowy evening—the take your breath away type of cold. I hurried into the warm store and took my time shuffling down the aisles. I found my few treasured gifts and went to the register to check out.

The man behind me put two Bibles on the conveyer belt. I looked at the Bibles and said, "Those are beautiful Bibles, and what a great price!" Note: these Bibles were thick, leather bound, study Bibles—drawing you to pick them up and open them simply by the cover alone!

He replied, "Yes, I ran out of Bibles for my Bible ministry, and I need to buy more." Immediately I asked, "What's your Bible ministry?" He humbly said, "I am a real estate agent, and I give Bibles to all of my clients and anyone else the Lord leads me to give one to. I keep them in my car so I always have them. But I just gave my last one away." With such excitement I said, "What a beautiful gift to give and what a ministry you have!" Suddenly the teenage cashier entered the conversation. She said, "I just bought a new journal Bible today, and I am so excited. I have been saving to get one!" Wow. Such excitement was in our hearts about giving, seeing, and receiving the greatest gift on earth—the Word of God.

I paid for my gifts that suddenly seemed as trivial as *The Muffin Man* nursery rhyme and went on my way, not with a new Bible but with a new conviction. Am I looking for opportunities to give the gift of Jesus and His Truth? Can I be on mission like the Bible man who is an everyday, everywhere Kingdom Laborer in the harvest fields looking for ways to give the gift of hope?

Look how valuable God's truth is:

- **"But He answered and said, 'It is written, 'Man shall not live by bread alone, but by every word that proceeds from the mouth of God.'" Matthew 4:4, NKJV**

- **"For whatever things were written before were written for our learning, that we through the patience and comfort of the Scriptures might have hope." Romans 15:4, NKJV**

- **"All Scripture is given by inspiration of God, and is profitable for doctrine, for reproof, for correction, for instruction in righteousness, that the man of God may be complete, thoroughly equipped for every good work." 2 Timothy 3:16-17, NKJV**

- **"For the word of God is living and powerful, and sharper than any two-edged sword, piercing even to the division of soul and spirit, and of joints and marrow, and is a discerner of the thoughts and intents of the heart. And there is no creature hidden from His sight, but all things are naked and open to the eyes of Him to whom we must give account." Hebrews 4:12-13, NKJV**

May the Lord reveal to us new ways to share His love and His truth. Perhaps I can combine the two and deliver fresh baked muffins and a Bible to someone God puts on my heart!

What would God have you do? There are endless ways to creatively share Jesus with others. Take time now and ask God for unique ways that you can share His love. Consider your career, passions, neighborhood, opportunities, and look for ways to encourage others! You may find it challenging, but it will certainly be rewarding!

How can you make Monumental Moments and live to multiply His movement today?

DAY 14: CALLED TO TESTIFY

Have you ever been called to testify as a witness in a court case? I am sure most of us have not. How about testifying on behalf of Jesus Christ? Have you shared your testimony of Jesus with others? We are all called to be His witnesses!

Isaiah 43:10-12 says,

"You are My witnesses," says the Lord, "And My servant whom I have chosen, that you may know and believe Me, and understand that I am He. Before Me there was no God formed, nor shall there be after Me. I, even I, am the Lord, and besides Me there is no savior. I have declared and saved, I have proclaimed, and there was no foreign god among you; therefore, you are My witnesses," says the Lord, "that I am God" (NKJV).

The Lord is challenging me more and more to be His witness—not just when I am called upon, but everywhere I go! Have you ever felt that way? We have been chosen. It takes intentionality and boldness at times to share, while other times, we can't help not to.

There is a story of Jesus cleansing a leper in Mark 1. Though Jesus asked the man not to say anything regarding this interaction because Jesus had more work to do in the city, the man simply couldn't contain it. He began to proclaim the news freely and spread it throughout the city. It was such a life-changing story that suddenly people started running from every direction out of the city into the deserted places to meet Jesus.

Let's look closer at this story! **Mark 1:40-45** says,

> **Now a leper came to Him, imploring Him, kneeling down to Him and saying to Him, "If You are willing, You can make me clean." Then Jesus, moved with compassion, stretched out His hand and touched him, and said to him, "I am willing; be cleansed." As soon as He had spoken, immediately the leprosy left him, and he was cleansed. And He strictly warned him and sent him away at once, and said to him, "See that you say nothing to anyone; but go your way, show yourself to the priest, and offer for your cleansing those things which Moses commanded, as a testimony to them." However, he went out and began to proclaim it freely, and to spread the matter, so that Jesus could no longer openly enter the city, but was outside in deserted places; and they came to Him from every direction.**

Imagine where you would be today, if someone didn't share Christ with you? You have a story to tell that God wants you to share with others! Don't hold back! There are people everywhere waiting to hear the Good News! It could change their life for eternity. Who is God asking you to share your God-Story with? Please don't miss or waste any opportunity! Decide today and be bold and courageous. God is with you!

How can you make Monumental Moments and live to multiply His movement today?

DAY 15: WATCH YOUR STEP

I was in a grocery store in Michigan recently picking up a few items to make dinner for my in-laws, who were needing a little extra help that week. I had my menu planned out, grocery list in hand, and was quickly moving through the aisles along with my husband filling the shopping cart. We were on a mission.

It happened to be late in the evening, so the aisles were relativity empty as most shoppers were already home for the night.

Bread, milk, fruit, vegetables, I checked the boxes off one by one in the note section of my phone and then decided to grab grandpa's favorite . . . ice cream! It didn't take long to realize we were grabbing lots of extra items beyond our list—par for the course with us.

We turned down the frozen food aisle to choose a sweet treat for grandpa before heading to the checkout. There was such a wide selection of ice cream—more than I was accustomed to at our smaller grocery store back home. Superman, Michigan Cherry, and Mackinac Island Fudge ice cream filled the shelves—sweet treats and tantalizing flavors native to the Midwest and hard to come by in other areas of the country. It was hard to choose the perfect flavor. We settled on Butter Pecan, his favorite!

Freezer case after freezer case lining both sides of the aisle were beautifully stocked and competing for my attention. But there was one thing that stood out above all else. It wasn't the merchandise or the variety of the ice cream flavors. It was the freezer units themselves and the specialty, smart lighting.

As I continued down the aisle, every single time I would get a few steps closer to the next freezer case, the dark display case would suddenly light up and completely light the walkway in front of me. The smart technology allowed the units to keep the lights off when no one was shopping but would brightly light up instantly when shoppers were nearby.

I smiled and couldn't help but think of **Psalm 119:105**, which says, **"Thy word is a lamp unto my feet, and a light unto my path" (KJV).**

It was as if God was physically lighting the path before me step by step. It was such a great visual of His promise! God desires us to be near Him and in His Word. He promises to be a lamp to our feet and light to our path!

Are you walking, watching, and believing God will lead your way and light your path? Take time today to ask the LORD to shine brightly and reveal next steps for you as you journey with Him. There is no greater path to take than His path!

How can you make Monumental Moments and live to multiply His movement today?

DAY 16: MEET GEORGE JETSON

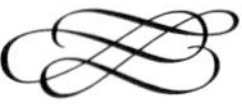

A refrigeration truck changing lanes on the way to deliver ice to their next stop; a diesel-powered school bus loaded with students stopped at another stop sign; an SUV leaving the restaurant loaded with business men and women carpooling back to the office; a convertible with girls laughing and bopping their heads to music at a stop light; an empty car with satellites and technology filling the roof driving through a busy intersection: one of these things *is not* like the other!

Imagine the surprise on my face when this girl from small town USA saw an empty vehicle passing in front of me at an intersection in Arizona. That's correct—no driver and no passengers in the vehicle, but a car that was driving through as usual. Not only that, but soon, I passed another car that was empty driving along beside me. Then, similar cars in various intersections and on random streets throughout town were continuing to pass me with still no people in the cars. It was a perplexing sight.

I did not see anyone in the vehicles. It felt like an episode that could be in a modern day *The Jetsons* cartoon with George and Jane. I kept thinking how unusual it was. It stood out amongst all the hustle and bustle of moving traffic from every direction. It grabbed my attention no doubt!

Like the Lord faithfully does, He challenged me through this real-life visual. I felt the Lord pose another question to me: *Do my disciples and Kingdom Laborers look different in this world? Can you spot them amongst the crowds?*

"Oh LORD, teach me how to shine brightly for you so that others may see something different. May they see you Jesus," I prayed.

Matthew 5:13-16 says,

You are the salt of the earth; but if the salt loses its flavor, how shall it be seasoned? It is then good for nothing but to be thrown out and trampled underfoot by men. You are the light of the world. A city that is set on a hill cannot be hidden. Nor do they light a lamp and put it under a basket, but on a lampstand, and it gives light to all who are in the house. Let your light so shine before men, that they may see your good works and glorify your Father in heaven (NKJV).

Kingdom Laborers, let your light shine brightly! How are you standing out for Christ amongst the crowds these days? Let's ask the Lord to help us to share Him everywhere we go! When people see us, may they see the love of God. May you look different because of the work of God in you.

How can you make Monumental Moments and live to multiply His movement today?

DAY 17: YAHWEH

YAHWEH, the Great I Am, we cry out to You!

The warfare happening in Israel and continually around the world is a horrific nightmare. Images and reports are nearly too much to bear. If we can't bear to witness or hear of it, how much worse for those living within it?

How can we help from nearly a world away? What can we do? We can pray. Will you commit to pray? We may not have the words, but He does!

Romans 8:26 tells us,

Likewise the Spirit also helps in our weaknesses. For we do not know what we should pray for as we ought, but the Spirit Himself makes intercession for us with groanings which cannot be uttered (NKJV).

We may not know how to fully pray, but we can pray scriptures! Will you position yourself to pray for the wars, rumors of wars, and the persecuted around the world? You may be the only one to lift up your voice on behalf of the broken or hurting that God has placed upon your heart.

Let's pray:

Peace

- **"Peace I leave with you, My peace I give to you; not as the world gives do I give to you. Let not your heart be troubled, neither let it be afraid." John 14:27, NKJV**

The Lord Will Fight the Battle

- **"And Moses said to the people, "Do not be afraid. Stand still, and see the salvation of the Lord, which He will accomplish for you today. For the Egyptians whom you see today, you shall see again no more forever. The Lord will fight for you, and you shall hold your peace." Exodus 14:13-14, NKJV**

Strength

- **"Fear not, for I am with you; be not dismayed, for I am your God. I will strengthen you, Yes, I will help you, I will uphold you with My righteous right hand." Isaiah 41:10, NKJV**

Courage

- **"Be strong and of good courage, do not fear nor be afraid of them; for the Lord your God, He *is* the One who goes with you. He will not leave you nor forsake you." Deuteronomy 31:6, NKJV**

Refuge

- **"He who dwells in the secret place of the Most High shall abide under the shadow of the Almighty. I will say of the Lord, "He is my refuge and my fortress; My God, in Him I will trust. Surely, He shall deliver you from the snare of the fowler and from the perilous pestilence. He shall cover you with His feathers, and under His wings you shall take refuge; His truth shall be your shield and buckler. You shall not be afraid of the terror by night, nor of the arrow that flies by day, nor of the pestilence that walks in darkness, nor of the destruction that lays waste at noonday." Psalm 91:1-6, NKJV**

Deliverance

- **"But as for me, my prayer is to You, O Lord, in the acceptable time; O God, in the multitude of Your mercy, hear me in the truth of Your salvation. Deliver me out of the mire and let me not sink; let me be delivered from those who hate me, and out of the deep waters. Let not the floodwater overflow me or let the deep swallow me up; and let not the pit shut its mouth on me. Hear me, O Lord, for Your loving kindness is good; turn to me according to the multitude of Your tender mercies. And do not hide Your face from Your servant, for I am in trouble; hear me speedily. Draw near to my soul and redeem it; deliver me because of my enemies." Psalm 69:13-18, NKJV**

When we lack words, we can pray the scriptures. Will you commit to making prayer a daily part of your life if you haven't already? Prayer is powerful. Prayer can change situations and circumstances.

No matter where you are in your prayer journey, will you commit to communicating with God more and going to war in prayer?

How can you make Monumental Moments and live to multiply His movement today?

DAY 18: THE ULTIMATE SACRIFICE

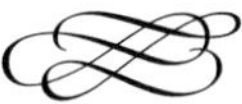

My husband and I were traveling and returning home to the Denver airport recently. As we were leaving our gate and headed toward baggage claim, we noticed a large crowd gathering around another gate waiting in anticipation for people to exit the plane from an incoming flight.

We decided to slow down and see what was transpiring. Rarely do large groups gather and watch intently like this at airports. I leaned in and asked one of the spectators what everyone was waiting for. She smiled and said, "This is an Honor Flight."

Not knowing exactly what that meant, I googled it to find out an Honor Flight is an opportunity for American Veterans to travel to Washington DC to visit monuments and memorials dedicated to their heroic military service.

Realizing how special this moment was, we stayed adding to the cheering section as the crowd clapped, whistled, and saluted American Veterans one by one disembarking the aircraft. Wheelchairs and canes accompanied many of the elderly men and women that were slowly exiting the plane.

These souls dedicated their lives and fought valiantly for freedom. I couldn't help but cry with thanksgiving and gratitude for their selfless sacrifice. Many waved back as tears ran down their weathered, wrinkled cheeks. One woman in her Vietnam Veteran hat even said, "This is a much better welcome home than the first time around."

Every single one of these brave men and women were willing to lay down their life for the freedom of others. Can you imagine their emotions during the battles and as they looked upon the monuments and memorials dedicated to their service and the many others who lost their lives? Often, they do not receive the fullness of the honor due.

It made me think of the One who gave His life so that none should perish. **John 3:16** says, **"For God so loved the world, that He gave His only Son, that whoever believes in Him should not perish but have eternal life."**

Christ willingly gave His life for all of mankind so every single person around the world could have freedom from sin and have eternal life. Are we honoring Christ for His selfless sacrifice?

1 Peter 3:15 says,

But in your hearts honor Christ the Lord as holy, always being prepared to make a defense to anyone who asks you for a reason for the hope that is in you; yet do it with gentleness and respect.

Take a moment today and thank Jesus Christ for the sacrifice He made for YOU. Look over the Romans Road again and memorize it! Share it with others that they may call upon the name of the Lord, repent, believe, and be saved!

- **"For all have sinned and fall short of the glory of God." Romans 3:23**

- **"For the wages of sin is death, but the free gift of God is eternal life in Christ Jesus our Lord." Romans 6:23**

- **"But God shows His love for us in that while we were still sinners, Christ died for us." Romans 5:8**

- **"Because, if you confess with your mouth that Jesus is Lord and believe in your heart that God raised Him from the dead, you will be saved. For with the heart, one believes and is justified, and with the mouth one confesses and is saved." Romans 10:9-10**

- **"For everyone who calls on the name of the Lord will be saved." Romans 10:13**

Where are you in your journey with God today? Are you honoring Christ for His selfless sacrifice? Pause and thank Him for freely giving His life and dying on the cross for your freedom from sin. He paid a debt we could never repay.

How can you make Monumental Moments and live to multiply His movement today?

DAY 19: FORGE FORWARD

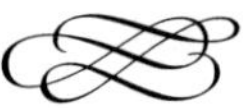

I believe within our very DNA there is a hunger in each of our hearts. There is something within us that is longing to know God and do something great for His Kingdom. After all, we are created in His image! We are created to be in relationship with God, our Creator. Sometimes, it just takes us a while to figure out it is God alone that was intended to fill the God-sized hole in our hearts!

The more I get to know God, the more I long to know Him more intimately and serve Him faithfully. I want to be a vessel He may use to advance His Kingdom. I want to forge forward in my relationship with Him and my service to Him. Have you felt that way as you continue to journey with God?

I was reading a social media post recently that started with the word "Forget." For whatever reason, my mind instantly translated the word to "Forge." I paused and thought that's interesting. Forge is the majority of the word "forget" with the letter "t" simply added at the end. Could the "t" be there at the end of the word to remind me that the cross will help me forget what is behind me and Forge forward to what is ahead?

Immediately, I thought of **Philippians 3:13-14,**

Brothers, I do not consider that I have made it my own. But one thing I do: forgetting what lies behind and straining forward to what lies ahead, I press on toward the goal for the prize of the upward call of God in Christ Jesus.

That's it! If we want to forge forward in God, we must forget what lies behind and our old, selfish ways. How do we do that? By the power of the cross! He alone is our Helper and our Sustainer. In Him we are a new creation. The old has gone, and the new has come!

He will arm and equip us for our new life in Him. Let's forge forward boldly and confidently in Him! Allow the cross to do its perfect work and help us forge"**t**" what is behind us, so we can forge forward to what lies ahead—pressing into the goal for the prize of the upward call of God in Christ Jesus!

Boldly forge forward this week through confidence in Christ—looking ahead because of the work of the cross.

What is it that you need to forget in order to forge forward in God? Pause and pray. God is listening.

How can you make Monumental Moments and live to multiply His movement today?

DAY 20: WHAT'S THE NAME?

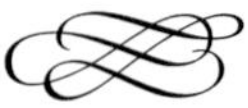

I stayed at a hotel recently while on an adventurous scuba diving vacation. As the wonderful week of fun in the sun came to an end, I found myself at the front desk asking for help scheduling an early cab to the airport for our 6 a.m. flight back to the U.S.

The kind assistant, eager to help, smiled and quickly called the taxi service requesting our cab for a crazy 3:45 a.m. pickup. It was going to be a rough night and an early morning. She politely answered the questions being asked on the other end of the line, and then paused.

She leaned over the counter, looked directly at me, and asked for my name to put on the reservation—expecting a quick and easy response. I smiled and said, "It's a long one. The name is Motschenbacher." She looked at me, and without hesitation said,

"Um, no." It was as if I was to immediately come up with a new last name! Being quick on my feet I said,

"Scott," which is my husband's first name. Clearly that was easy enough to work with and acceptable. She proceeded to continue in conversation on the phone.

As I reflected on the moment, I questioned myself, "How often have I substituted my identity as a Christian either intentionally or unintentionally? Do I stand and declare who I am even when it's inconvenient, when I'm misunderstood, when it's hard to comprehend, or when it takes a while to explain? What about you?

The Lord has gone from calling us servants to calling us friends. As children of God, you and I are now friends of God. Our identity is in Him! We have a new identity as Christians we must be proud to stand for!

John 15:15 says,

No longer do I call you servants, for the servant does not know what his master is doing; but I have called you friends, for all that I have heard from My Father I have made known to you.

Friend of God, let's not be ashamed of our identity or shrink back providing substitutes to fit situations! As a Christian, be proud of the name you carry and represent! He paid a hefty price for you to bear His name! Declare today who He says that you are.

How can you make Monumental Moments and live to multiply His movement today?

DAY 21: THAT'S A NICE BOULDER

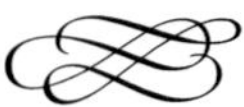

When my kids were younger, they used to love to watch animated movies. One of their favorite movies from the early 2000s was Shrek. They had favorite scenes in the movie they just couldn't wait to see and usually the scenes revolved around Donkey!

One scene they put on repeat—constantly stopping, rewinding, and rewatching. This scene was when Donkey is walking with Shrek through the forest and comes upon Shrek's modest home for the first time.

As the scene played over and over, I continually heard this: "I like that boulder. That is a nice boulder," as Donkey tried to back pedal from previous comments about Shrek's home! The quote would often echo throughout our home laced with giggles and copycat repeats from my children.

"That is a nice boulder," is an interesting comment, isn't it? Often people don't recognize rocks and boulders at first glance.

I was reading in **Mark 16** lately, and I read about a large boulder, but not a welcomed one.

Mark 16:1-8 says,

> **When the Sabbath was past, Mary Magdalene, Mary the mother of James, and Salome bought spices, so that they might go and anoint Him. And very early on the first day of the week, when the sun had risen, they went to the tomb. And they were saying to one another, "Who will roll away the stone for us from the entrance of the tomb?" And looking up, they saw that the stone had been rolled back—it was very large. And entering the tomb, they saw a young man sitting on the right side, dressed in a white robe, and they were alarmed. And he said to them, "Do not be alarmed. You seek Jesus of Nazareth, who was crucified. He has risen; He is not here. See the place where they laid Him. But go, tell His disciples and Peter that He is going before you to Galilee. There you will see Him, just as He told you." And they went out and fled from the tomb, for trembling and astonishment had seized them, and they said nothing to anyone, for they were afraid.**

At this time, people realized Jesus was crucified, died on the cross, was buried, and a large stone had been rolled in front of the tomb. When the Sabbath had passed, as soon as they could, at sunrise, three compassionate women gathered to purchase spices and go to the tomb together to anoint the lifeless body of Jesus.

In reading this story for many years, I never really caught the timing, urgency and even the conversation that was happening with the women on the way to the tomb that morning. In conversation they asked, "Who will roll away the stone for us from the entrance of the tomb?" It is documented in this scripture that it was a very large stone. I am sure this was a huge boulder.

I doubt the women were found saying, "That is a nice boulder." As you probably already know, stones, large rocks, and boulders can be extravagantly heavy—especially stones large enough to cover an entrance of a tomb! The women were trying to create a plan on their way to the tomb with their valued, newly purchased spices to get inside and anoint the precious body of Jesus.

As they looked up, they saw the stone had already been rolled away. Imagine their amazement and confusion. They were just talking about who was going to move this boulder. Then, they look up and see the stone has already been rolled away. They learn Jesus is no longer there but has risen from the dead!

Scripture says they fled from the tomb as trembling and astonishment seized them. They went from devising a plan to move a boulder to get to Jesus, to fleeing in astonishment after a young man in the tomb told them Jesus was not there.

Have you ever been faced with heavy things that seem virtually impossible to move—wondering how on earth you can move them? Are there boulders in your life keeping you from Jesus that you need to pray for Him to remove?

It's time to look up, raise your gaze, and know through the power of His resurrection, the stone has been rolled away! He has made a way for you to have direct access to Him. Let's examine and ask the Lord how He can remove the boulders in our life that are keeping us at a distance from Him. Look up and focus on the King of Kings in the fullness of His resurrected glory!

Remind yourself of the sacrifice, price that was paid, and redeeming love that tore the veil and rolled the stone away to remove the barriers between you and the Lord!

How can you make Monumental Moments and live to multiply His movement today?

DAY 22: BELLS AND BOWLS

I was reading in the book of Zechariah recently. In **Zechariah 14:20 (NKJV)** there is a term in all caps, "**HOLINESS TO THE LORD.**" It's as if the phrase is written as a 3D image jumping off the page of the Bible, and we do not need 3D glasses to see it. I couldn't help but stop, stare, and pray in awe and wonder. HOLINESS TO THE LORD in all caps? Clearly Zechariah wanted to make a point.

Zechariah 14:20-21 says,

In that day "HOLINESS TO THE LORD"'shall be engraved on the bells of the horses. The pots in the Lord's house shall be like the bowls before the altar. Yes, every pot in Jerusalem and Judah shall be holiness to the Lord of hosts. Everyone who sacrifices shall come and take them and cook in them. In that day there shall no longer be a Canaanite in the house of the Lord of hosts (NKJV).

We can read scriptures at various times or seasons in our lives, and they hit us differently. I have read that scripture before I am sure, but this time it was different. Have you had verses, words, or phrases in the Bible grab your attention? HOLINESS TO THE LORD captured mine that day.

I questioned, "HOLINESS TO THE LORD" will be engraved on the bells of horses? And the pots in the Lord's house will be like bowls before the alter—all will be HOLINESS TO THE LORD?

In the day of the Lord, when He returns, everything will be made holy—even down to common items like pots in a kitchen and bells on bridles.

Knowing that truth, then, what about me now? What about us? Are we setting our lives apart now as "HOLINESS TO THE LORD?" God is holy and everything in His Kingdom will one day reflect HOLINESS TO THE LORD.

I believe the Lord wants to continue to keep this concept, phrase, and image ever before us just like the prominent inscription at the front of the altar in Hughes Auditorium at Asbury that was on display for the world to see through the Asbury Revival!

How can your life better reflect HOLINESS TO THE LORD? We are all a work in progress. We have countless choices and decisions to make every day, and they will either honor or dishonor the Lord. As people look at you, do they see HOLINESS TO THE LORD?

How can you make Monumental Moments and live to multiply His movement today?

DAY 23: DO IT AGAIN DAD

There was a popular commercial that debuted in 1989. The commercial started by capturing the audience's attention with sweet music. As viewers were lured into the screen, they saw, off into the distance, a father and daughter sitting patiently, side-by-side, gazing at the sun setting into the horizon. The sky lit up with amazing hues of vibrant yellows and oranges, and the father said, "Ah, there goes the sun." After a slight pause he continued, "Going, going, gone." The sweet, young daughter turned and adoringly looked at her father, and almost whispering, said, "Do it again, Daddy!"

It was a short and sweet, wholesome commercial by Life Savers candy. I still remember the commercial today like I did the first night it caught my attention on the large, bubble television. It was a "feel-good" commercial. Nowadays, when I desire a dose of nostalgia, I throw Life Savers candy in my cart at the grocery store. It's almost like I relive the sunset commercial every time I pull a new, sunset color of candy out of the waxy packaging!

Beautiful sunsets have a way of stopping us in our tracks, don't they? If only they could last just a little longer. But after just a few moments, they disappear like a vapor. I had the rare opportunity to see my first-ever, 1-hour sunset recently. The sky was electrifying.

There were shades of purples, yellows, reds, oranges, and blues that I don't think I have ever seen before. I was on a flight, headed west from Florida to Texas. By chance, I happened to sit in a window seat on the correct side of the plane that night.

As the plane took off, I was captivated by the spectacular sunset over the Gulf of Mexico. I couldn't stop looking out the tiny airplane window. I lost track of time as the colors continued to hold my gaze. Suddenly, I realized this was the longest, unhindered sunset I have ever experienced! For an hour, I saw remnants of the sunset as the airplane, traveling nearly 600 miles per hour, chased the setting sun.

It was a moment, actually an hour, I will never forget! It made me think of the time in the Bible where the Lord made the sun stand still for Joshua and the Mighty Men of Valor as they fought in battle.

We can read about it in **Joshua 10:12-13,**

> **At that time Joshua spoke to the Lord in the day when the Lord gave the Amorites over to the sons of Israel, and he said in the sight of Israel, "Sun, stand still at Gibeon, and moon, in the Valley of Aijalon." And the sun stood still, and the moon stopped, until the nation took vengeance on their enemies. Is this not written in the Book of Jashar? The sun stopped in the midst of heaven and did not hurry to set for about a whole day. There has been no day like it before or since, when the Lord heeded the voice of a man, for the Lord fought for Israel.**

As I thought about this scripture that says, "**The sun stopped in the midst of heaven and did not hurry to set for about a whole day. There has been no day like it before or since, when the Lord heeded the voice of a man, for the Lord fought for Israel,**" I couldn't help but thank God for being our Ever-Present Help in Time of Need. He is our Defender. He is our Shield. He is our Source. He fights for us. God hears us!

As I continued to reflect on my extended glimpse of the almost never-ending sunset, it had me questioning myself. How often am I praying? What am I praying and believing God for? Am I praying mountain-moving, sun-stand-still prayers? Am I expectant for God to move? Am I watching in faith for His miracles? I need to pray more! I need to pray and believe in faith that God will move! I need to pray for things that seem impossible. I need to pray Kingdom-advancing prayers!

What are you praying, believing, and waiting in faith for? God is fighting for you! There are beautiful miracles God has in store! Stay expectant. Increase your faith. Ask the Lord Almighty to align you and your prayers with His heart! Then, watch for the *Son* to move!

How can you make Monumental Moments and live to multiply His movement today?

DAY 24: CAN YOU GIVE ME A HAND?

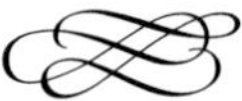

"I slept like a baby," isn't something you will hear me say often. I usually do not sleep well. In addition, I have learned through the years to ask the Lord to help me be sensitive to Him even if he wants to speak in the middle of the night!

I woke up one night in recent weeks not to a voice, but to a simple image. I saw a set of confidently positioned, cupped hands in white gloves holding an extravagantly large, beautiful, flawless diamond. The diamond was huge, like the size of a softball, and perfectly cut. It was brilliant! Everything in me wanted to jump and take hold of this treasure. It was as if the Lord was giving a visual of the incredible Kingdom treasures He has to gift each of us.

Looking beyond the diamond, I couldn't help but notice the white gloves holding the glistening treasure. I knew these brilliant white gloves represented a servant's heart. And, I had an awareness of the need to properly handle the precious and priceless gift.

This image reminded me of **Matthew 13:44** which says,

Again, the kingdom of heaven is like treasure hidden in a field,

which a man found and hid; and for joy over it he goes and sells all that he has and buys that field" (NKJV).

Oh, we have treasures in Him! But what are we going to do with those treasures? With great joy, do we do everything we can to accept and receive the treasures? We wouldn't leave a hidden treasure we found without doing everything in our power to take it with us. Lottery winners don't decide to walk away from claiming their winning ticket.

There are so many treasures to find in God. Are we seeking Him? Are we eagerly receiving them—salvation, wisdom, discernment, peace, hope, love, joy, blessings, and so much more? Once we have received these treasures, what will we do with them? Will we keep them, make room for them, and steward them? Will we share them, or will we hoard them? Friends, we must share these treasures with the world!

As I prayed and continued to see this beautiful image, it was almost as if I could see this extravagant diamond treasure being handed over with a transfer of ownership to others. The Kingdom-treasure transfer from sturdy hands in white, servant gloves was confidently being received by hands in a variety of other gloves.

The diamond transfer was received with hands in garden gloves, driving gloves, medical gloves, food-service gloves, cleaning gloves, golf gloves, baseball gloves, work gloves, scuba diving gloves, winter gloves, sailing gloves, dirt bike riding gloves, weightlifting gloves, and gloves I had never seen before. As I saw these gloves holding Kingdom treasures, I thought of the hefty weight and responsibility we have as Kingdom Laborers to share these treasures with others in the variety of harvest fields!

The Apostle Paul sure did everything he could to share Kingdom treasures with everyone! He became all things to all men!

In **1 Corinthians 9:19-23** he says,

For though I am free from all men, I have made myself a servant to all, that I might win the more; and to the Jews I became as a Jew, that I might win Jews; to those who are under the law, as under the law, that I might win those who are under the law; to those who are without law, as without law (not being without law toward God, but under law toward Christ), that I might win those who are without law; to the weak I became as weak, that I might win the weak. I have become all things to all men, that I might by all means save some. Now this I do for the Gospel's sake, that I may be partaker of it with you" (NKJV).

We must get our gloves dirty, friends! Let's go into all the harvest fields! Listen to how Jesus put it in **Matthew 9:37-38** in the Message version,

Then Jesus made a circuit of all the towns and villages. He taught in their meeting places, reported kingdom news, and healed their diseased bodies, healed their bruised and hurt lives. When He looked out over the crowds, His heart broke. So confused and aimless they were, like sheep with no shepherd. "What a huge harvest!" He said to His disciples. "How few workers! On your knees and pray for harvest hands!"

We are His harvest hands! But Jesus is telling us to get on our knees and pray for MORE Harvest Hands! Will you be in the baseball fields, medical offices, golf courses, gardens, kitchens, and beyond as the hands and feet of Jesus, laboring for Him? Let's pray for more harvest hands and Kingdom Laborers! You have Kingdom treasures in your hands! Share them with the world!

How can you make Monumental Moments and live to multiply His movement today?

DAY 25: HEY ALEXA

Do you have a question and need an answer? Chances are pretty good you can have an answer in mere seconds in many cases. Perhaps these days you are quickly turning to Alexa, Siri, or Google out of habit to get answers to your questions! Virtual assistants with voice recognition powered by artificial intelligence (AI) can give us an immediate answer to almost anything anymore!

My husband and I have been in such a habit recently of turning to Alexa to play music or get an overview of the weather pattern. It's just become a natural part of our daily routine anymore. In fact, at one point we went outside after asking Alexa what the weather was for the day, and I heard Scott mistakenly call the neighbor's dog Alexa! Laughing out loud literally at the moment, I realized "Alexa, okay Google, and hey Siri" are a natural part of our vocabulary anymore. It's amazing how quickly these virtual assistants respond to our voice and obey our commands. They are constantly at our service and beck and call.

As I continued laughing at Scott for calling the neighbor's dog Alexa, I thought to myself, "Oh Lord, are these crazy AI assistants more obedient to my voice and command than I am to you?"

It's a fair and honest question to ask, "Do these electronic devices respond quicker and with more accuracy than I do to the Lord Almighty, Creator of Heaven and Earth?"

How about you? Are you quick to respond when you hear the Lord speak to you or ask something of you? Do you have your voice recognition on high alert to be waiting for God's promptings?

May the Lord help us as Kingdom Laborers to be sensitive to His voice and quick to respond in full surrender and obedience!

The word of God encourages us:

- **"I hasten and do not delay to keep Your commandments." Psalm 119:60**
- **"My sheep hear My voice, and I know them, and they follow Me." John 10:27**
- **"And your ears shall hear a word behind you, saying, 'This is the way, walk in it,' when you turn to the right or when you turn to the left." Isaiah 30:21**
- **"Why do you call me 'Lord, Lord,' and not do what I tell you? Everyone who comes to Me and hears My words and does them, I will show you what he is like: he is like a man building a house, who dug deep and laid the foundation on the rock. And when a flood arose, the stream broke against that house and could not shake it, because it had been well built. But the one who hears and does not do them is like a man who built a house on the ground without a foundation. When the stream broke against it, immediately it fell, and the ruin of that house was great." Luke 6:46-49**

Perhaps you want to take a moment and ask God to forgive you for not being sensitive to His voice. Ask Him to help you know His voice above all others and to be quick to respond!

How can you make Monumental Moments and live to multiply His movement today?

DAY 26: DO YOU HEAR WHAT I HEAR?

Oh, the sweet, sweet sound of a harmonizing choir with chords and progressions taking you on a melodic journey. There is so much to take in with layers and layers of rich melody and the ups and downs of crescendos and diminuendos! Do you know the experience I am describing?

Perhaps you have encountered it with Christmas carolers at your door, attending a musical, singing in a choir, or when listening to music on the radio. It can often be so captivating you want to burst forth into song too! There is just something about music that gets everyone's attention.

Imagine the surprise of the shepherds standing in the dark, quiet fields as suddenly they were surrounded by a multitude of heavenly hosts praising God—some of the first Christmas carolers on earth!

Luke 2:7-14 describes the moment,

And she brought forth her firstborn Son, and wrapped Him in swaddling cloths, and laid Him in a manger, because there was no room for them in the inn. Now there were in the same country shepherds living out in the fields, keeping watch over their flock

> **by night. And behold, an angel of the Lord stood before them, and the glory of the Lord shone around them, and they were greatly afraid. Then the angel said to them, "Do not be afraid, for behold, I bring you good tidings of great joy which will be to all people. For there is born to you this day in the city of David a Savior, who is Christ the Lord. And this will be the sign to you: You will find a Babe wrapped in swaddling cloths, lying in a manger." And suddenly there was with the angel a multitude of the heavenly host praising God and saying: "Glory to God in the highest, and on earth peace, goodwill toward men" (NKJV)!**

Can you imagine that moment? Shepherds living out in fields were simply tending to their sheep watching over them in the dark, cool evening. As the sun was setting, they must have thought it was a night like any other. They probably went through the motions of their normal, nightly routines like many of us often do. Until suddenly an Angel of the Lord appeared and stood in front of them and God's glory encircled them.

The scripture says, they were greatly afraid. I'm sure I would have been too. What about you? But the Angel of the Lord encouraged them and gave them insight regarding what was to come. And while the Angel of the Lord was there speaking to them, suddenly an angelic choir, a multitude showed up praising God. They entered the scene praising.

Will you join in this melodic adventure with the multitude of heavenly host and praise God saying, "Glory to God in the highest, and on earth peace, goodwill toward men?" Will your life be a posture of praise?

Praising God and giving Him glory is more than a one-time occurrence. May our lives continually praise Him! Let's go from hearing about the praise or listening to the praise to helping lead the praise for the King of Kings!

How can you make Monumental Moments and live to multiply His movement today?

DAY 27: HELP! I'VE FALLEN, AND I CAN'T GET UP

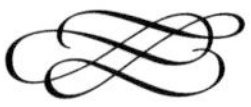

You should have seen it! So caught off guard, I didn't know if I should laugh or cry.

It was around 8:30 p.m. on a Monday evening at a restaurant in Colorado. Three women walked into this restaurant together and stood by the hostess stand, patiently waiting to be seated at a table. The next thing you know, they were on their way across the restaurant, but it was not a casual stroll. Like train cars, they followed closely behind each other.

Then, there was the moment worth waiting for, where all the restaurant guests had front row seats. The woman at the end of the line in her cute, high heeled booties slipped on the polished cement pavement. Throwing her arms out as if she was surfing, she got her balance only to slip again step after step, nearly wiping out. But with her cat-like reflexes, she saved the day and stood upright. By now, she had everyone's attention in the restaurant. It was such a spectacle it even had folks that were glued to the television sets now turned around and more interested in the local, impromptu entertainment than what was on the screens.

This woman seemed to gain her composure for a few steps, but as they say . . . the third time is a charm! She almost wiped out again. Still sliding all over the floor, but this time screaming too, she grabbed the closest thing near her—the woman in front her. It was a wrestling match to not go down. By this time, both women were sweating, screaming, and trying their best to stay upright. As I mentioned, it was a sight to see.

I must confess, I am the woman who couldn't walk a straight line in those cute, little, black boots. I was a train wreck. I almost wiped out on the slippery floor—not once, not twice, but three times. I was desperately reaching for anything to help me not fall to the ground. What's even worse . . . I had just met these women in person for the first time about one hour prior! You could say this wasn't one of my best moments.

I went on to have appetizers with these new God-fearing women to connect more, and of course, apologize over and over. During our conversations, you can bet I was thinking through my exit strategy of how I was going to walk back out of the restaurant without falling in about an hour!

Here is yet again another one of God's teaching moments for me. To put this night into context, I met these women in a church about an hour prior as we were all working together to refine our preaching and storytelling skills. I was up on the stage, behind a pulpit, preaching to a small group just an hour earlier. The next thing I knew, I was falling all over the place creating a scene at a restaurant next door. What a trip!

On the way home, as I relived the scene in my head, I felt the Lord remind me of a precious scripture in **Revelation 2:4**. I started reciting the scripture in my head, "**Remember how far you have fallen**." One minute I was preaching God's word and literally almost the next I was falling all over the place. As soon as I got home for the night, I pulled out my Bible to read **Revelation 2:4-5**,

> **Nevertheless I have this against you, that you have left your first love. Remember therefore from where you have fallen; repent and do the first works, or else I will come to you quickly and remove your lampstand from its place—unless you repent (NKJV).**

This was a great reminder we can be preaching, serving, and loving God one minute, and falling away the next. We must remember our first love (the LORD) and repent for our wayward acts. I don't want to be spiritually floundering through life. I want to be found continually hand in hand with my first love!

P.S. I did make it out of the restaurant that night without falling. But I will admit, I did pray without ceasing and shuffle my way all the way to the front door as I looked for chairs and tables to grab every step of the way!

May our spiritual journey with the Lord be rooted on solid, holy ground as we walk hand in hand with Him. Let's step up and repent when we fall! He is our strength and our source! May He always be our first love!

Have you fallen away? Do you need to step up and repent? Are you walking in the fullness of what God has for you? Take a minute and ask the Lord to help steady your feet and ignite your heart!

How can you make Monumental Moments and live to multiply His movement today?

DAY 28: GLOW IN THE DARK

It was very early one morning—honestly too early to be awake. I rolled over in the still of the night, surprised to see something glowing in the dark. My husband was wide awake, and though the room was still very dark, his face was brightly illuminated —like a glow-in-the-dark object. Somewhat disturbed that my sleep was interrupted, I asked him in a rather short tone of voice, "What are you doing?" In his not-so-short tone of voice, he simply and quietly replied,

"I'm reading my Bible."

He was in his Bible app reading God's Word on his phone, and his face nearly lit up the room! How could I argue with that? I am thankful I have a husband who loves the Word of God. There were many nights early in our marriage where he hadn't yet given His life to God, and I was praying almost continually for Him to surrender His life to Christ.

Suddenly, it was like a light bulb went on in my head. This was another precious moment and fulfillment of so many prayers I prayed years prior. I paused, sitting in the shadows, to check my attitude and thank God that I was waking up next to a husband that seeks God even in the stillness of night. Here we are, many years later, and he still loves the Word of God! What a beautiful and precious gift to be transformed by the Word and to watch others experience the same transformation!

God shed more light on the scriptures, and I stayed awake replaying the account of **Exodus 34** when Moses went up Mount Sinai to meet the LORD on the mountaintop early in the morning. This was also when God carved out the Ten Commandments on stone tablets for the second time.

Scripture says in **Exodus 34:29-35,**

> **When Moses came down from Mount Sinai with the two tablets of the covenant law in his hands, he was not aware that his face was radiant because he had spoken with the Lord. When Aaron and all the Israelites saw Moses, his face was radiant, and they were afraid to come near him. But Moses called to them; so, Aaron and all the leaders of the community came back to him, and he spoke to them. Afterward all the Israelites came near him, and he gave them all the commands the Lord had given him on Mount Sinai. When Moses finished speaking to them, he put a veil over his face. But whenever he entered the Lord's presence to speak with Him, he removed the veil until he came out. And when he came out and told the Israelites what he had been commanded, they saw that his face was radiant. Then Moses would put the veil back over his face until he went in to speak with the Lord (NIV).**

No, my husband is not Moses. But what a great visual and spiritual representation I got to see that morning of the transforming power of the Word of God that radiates and illuminates Christ in us!

Spending time with God and reading the Bible transforms us. Are you intentional to be in God's Word daily? He will make your soul radiant!

Matthew 5:16 says, "**In the same way, let your light shine before**

others, that they may see your good deeds and glorify your Father in heaven" (NIV)!

Let God's light in you shine brightly! May others see God's radiance in you as you spend time with the LORD!

How can you make Monumental Moments and live to multiply His movement today?

DAY 29: A MISSING PUZZLE PIECE

I remember visiting my grandmother's home as a child. There are so many fond memories. It seemed as though there was always a pot of green beans on the stove simmering in bacon grease and the smell of fresh, baked, buttermilk cornbread lingering in the air!

As we would drop in for unannounced visits to say hello, we would walk past a small table with puzzle pieces waiting to be put together. I can still hear my grandmother say, "Don't run off just yet. Let's go work a puzzle!" That's such a fun memory I have of grandma and a tradition I have brought out around the holidays!

It seems there is more time to "work a puzzle" like grandma said around the holidays as family and friends gather near. I try to take it to the next level and buy the hardest puzzle I can find, which doesn't go over well with my family!

As the years go by and my eyes get older, it's getting a bit harder to see the detail on the small puzzle pieces! This year, as I spent more time trying to study the puzzle pieces to find their perfect fit, I noticed I had a magnifying glass as a decoration on my bookshelf. I thought to myself, *This is going to come in handy!* I grabbed the magnifying glass and used it to see the puzzle pieces with such clarity and magnification. What relief it brought my tired and weary eyes!

Do you know that feeling I am talking about—the moment that suddenly something is magnified in such a way you can see all the details with such clarity? It's almost as if you can hear your own sigh of relief.

As I was holding the large magnifying glass, I couldn't help but think of Mary in **Luke, chapter 1,** of the Bible when she said, **"My soul magnifies the Lord."** I began to question, *Does my soul and life magnify the Lord? When others look at me, is Jesus magnified?*

What if we all paused and asked ourselves, *Are we magnifying the Lord, and can we magnify God further still with our life?*

God's word says this:

- **"Oh, magnify the Lord with me, and let us exalt His name together." Psalm 34:3, NKJV**

- **"And Mary said: 'My soul magnifies the Lord, and my spirit has rejoiced in God my Savior.'" Luke 1:46-47, NKJV**

- **"I will praise the name of God with a song and will magnify Him with thanksgiving." Psalm 69:30, NKJV**

As Kingdom Laborers, let's look for opportunities to magnify God for the world to see Jesus with such clarity and precision! Do you have a way you can magnify Him today?

How can you make Monumental Moments and live to multiply His movement today?

DAY 30: THE FRAGRANCE

"There they made Him a supper; and Martha served, but Lazarus was one of those who sat at the table with Him. Then Mary took a pound of very costly oil of spikenard, anointed the feet of Jesus, and wiped His feet with her hair. And the house was filled with the fragrance of the oil." John 12:2, NKJV

Can you even imagine watching a woman sitting at the feet of Jesus while He was at a dining table with others enjoying a meal? Can you see yourself looking on as she was anointing His well-traveled feet that had walked many miles—watching the movement of her beautiful, probably long hair that may have even been damp with fresh tears? What a sight to see.

The Scripture intricately describes the scene so well. I often ask myself, where would I be at this moment? Would I be hosting and serving, would I be at the table with Jesus, would I be sitting on the sidelines, would I be preoccupied and not even there, or would I be at His feet?

Not only can we see what happened, we can gain an even better understanding of the atmosphere as the Bible describes the smell.

It says the house was filled with the fragrance of costly spikenard oil. I know this . . . it takes a very fragrant oil, a very large amount, and a decent amount of time to fill a house with a fragrance. I can have candles on or an essential oil diffuser for hours before it penetrates the home and fills the house.

Sweet Mary must have tarried at Jesus' feet as the fragrant perfume permeated the air. Did the fragrance linger even longer after Mary stepped away and Jesus left? It certainly must have.

I wonder, does the amount of time I spend at the feet of Jesus saturate the atmosphere around me? I want the time I spend with the Lord to honor Him, be life changing for me and life giving for others around me. What is the aroma lingering within your home, car, workplace, and areas you frequent? Is it God honoring?

Now is a great time to make the necessary changes as you serve the King! Let's allow our time with the Lord to leave a sweet-smelling aroma everywhere we go!

How can you make Monumental Moments and live to multiply His movement today?

DAY 31: WHAT TAKES US SO LONG?

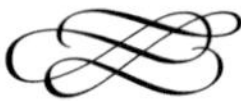

I long for my heart to echo the heartbeat of God. I want to rejoice in what He rejoices in and have my heart break when His heart breaks. I believe that happens as we continue to walk with the Lord and are made more and more into His image.

As I read the book of Genesis in the Bible, I have been wondering why Adam and Eve did not repent to God immediately after they disobeyed God in the garden. As I kept reading, I saw a pattern where Cain, their son, did not repent to God either, but rather became angry with God for not accepting his sacrifice. How long did it take for this sinful pattern and rebellion to stop with someone standing up and calling upon God? The Word of God tells us!

Do you ever get to the genealogy in the Bible and find yourself quickly skimming over it? I have. But I have also learned there is purpose in all of it.

Genesis 4:25-26 says,

And Adam knew his wife again, and she bore a son and called his name Seth, for she said, "God has appointed for me another offspring instead of Abel, for Cain killed him." To Seth also a son

was born, and he called his name Enosh. At that time people began to call upon the name of the Lord.

Man began to call upon the name of the Lord when Enosh was born. But, how long was that after Adam and Eve were created? Well, the Bible tells us that too! Let's keep reading. **Genesis 5:3-6** says,

When Adam had lived 130 years, he fathered a son in his own likeness, after his image, and named him Seth. The days of Adam after he fathered Seth were 800 years; and he had other sons and daughters. Thus all the days that Adam lived were 930 years, and he died. When Seth had lived 105 years, he fathered Enosh.

So we know Adam was 130 years old when he fathered Seth, and Seth was 105 years old when he fathered Enosh. 235 years and three generations later man began to call upon the name of the Lord.

I pray we are a people slow to sin and quick to repent—that we are not people who wait years or generations to call upon the name of the Lord. Christ gave everything, but often we do not want to sacrifice anything. Many pray for revival but want to disregard repentance.

I know God longs for us to turn from sin, repent, and walk in the fullness of what He has for us! Repentance should be a lifestyle as we walk with the Lord!

What does repentance look like? It's simply a broken heart before God asking for forgiveness for sin and disobedience. I believe it looks a lot like **Psalm 51**. King David had committed adultery with Bathsheba and cries out for mercy to God after he sins, and we read about it in **Psalm 51**! Let's spend some time in God's Word this week and read **Psalm 51**. Let's ask God to search our hearts, purge us, and wash us clean from the sin within our hearts!

What does repentance look like for you? Ask God to search your heart and wash you clean of sinful bents and patterns of disobedience.

How can you make Monumental Moments and live to multiply His movement today?

DAY 32: ARE YOU AHEAD OR BEHIND?

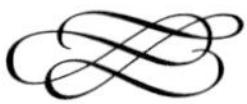

FOMO they call it—Fear Of Missing Out. In today's world, people are becoming more and more fearful of committing to anything because they are afraid something better may come up along the way. I am guilty. I have done that to some degree, but in a slightly different way. For quite some time now, my husband, Scott, and I have wanted to commit to a small group, life group, community group, etc., whatever you would like to call it. We simply want to grow deeper in community with fellow, like-minded believers as we journey through life!

The truth is, Scott's job has him traveling often. It's been that way for over 10 years now. We realize there would be many weeks we would not be able to attend meetings due to being out of town. Focusing on all the times we would miss the gathering has kept us crippled and stagnant in the world of small groups. I have realized, we are not the only ones thinking this way.

I was listening to several women talk about a Bible study they were considering. As they processed, they felt they were not going to commit because they would be missing several sessions due to prior commitments. Suddenly, the Lord put a spotlight on me. I felt like the Holy Spirit whispered to my heart: *As you refuse to commit to a 3- or 4-*

month long small group because you are focusing on the times you will miss, you need to know you are losing out on far more than the actual weeks you are missing.

In other words, if we have a 16-week group gathering and we miss four weeks, are we four weeks behind, or are we 12 weeks ahead?

Then, as God faithfully does, He showed me the truth in His Word. The enemy is so crafty and wants to hinder us and hold us back. He wants us to focus on what we do not have or will not have over what we can have!

Genesis 2:15-17 says,

> **The Lord God took the man and put him in the garden of Eden to work it and keep it. And the Lord God commanded the man, saying, "You may surely eat of every tree of the garden, but of the tree of the knowledge of good and evil you shall not eat, for in the day that you eat of it you shall surely die."**

God started out in the beginning by telling man all the things he could freely have. Then he gave direction on what to stay away from, why, and what the consequence would be. The devil quickly goes to work.

Genesis 3:1-5 says,

> **Now the serpent was more crafty than any other beast of the field that the Lord God had made. He said to the woman, "Did God actually say, 'You shall not eat of any tree in the garden?'" And the woman said to the serpent, "We may eat of the fruit of the trees in the garden, but God said, 'You shall not eat of the fruit of the tree that is in the midst of the garden, neither shall you touch it, lest you die.'" But the serpent said to the woman, "You will not surely die. For God knows that when you eat of it your eyes will be opened, and you will be like God, knowing good and evil."**

The devil created a distorted view for Eve—making her look at what she didn't have. Instead, there was life, joy, protection, provision, safety, and so much more in what God was offering and providing to her and Adam in the Garden of Eden.

What has God put before you to enjoy and take part in that the enemy is causing you to miss out on because He is making you focus on what you don't have, can't have, or are missing? Yes, we certainly want to be committed, to be all-in, and to let our "Yes" be "Yes."

If times arise that we can't participate due to life's circumstances, I believe we would be further ahead missing out on a portion of His abundance rather than not entering it at all because of FOMO.

How can you make Monumental Moments and live to multiply His movement today?

DAY 33: IS IT OBVIOUS?

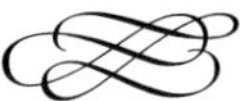

Some things are just obvious! Teens in wet bathing suits at the beach . . . most likely have been in the ocean or the lake. Trees dropping their leaves as the weather cools . . . most likely have us entering winter months. A vibrant red sky in the morning over ocean waves . . . most likely alerts storms on the horizon. Beautiful church bells chiming a melodic tune followed by 12 consecutive chimes . . . most likely alerts passersby it's noon and lunch time. Scrolling "Possible Spam Call" on your phone as it rings or vibrates . . . most likely alerts you to unknown telemarketers. Trophies, ribbons, and awards . . . most likely identify winners or champions. The list goes on.

Many things are obvious and recognizable in our world. Is it obvious we are Christians? Are we standing for Truth? Can others recognize we are believers? The disciples were recognizable. I think of Peter in **Matthew 26:69-74** after Jesus had been arrested. A young servant girl sees Peter in the courtyard and recognizes him as being with Jesus. Later, when Peter went out by the gate, another woman recognized him as being with **"Jesus the Nazarene."** Later still, others said to Peter, **"You really are one of them, since even your accent gives you away."**

In these references, people were referring to Peter physically being with Jesus. I pray as we spend time with our resurrected Lord, it's recognizable by everyone we encounter. I pray even strangers can say, "You really are one of them. You have been with Jesus." I pray we would be known by our Christlike words and deeds, and when others see us, they see Jesus. May our walk with the Lord lead others to Christ!

Please take time and review **Acts 4:1-22** for the full context, but the boldness of the disciples left people undeniably recognizing they had been with Jesus. **Acts 4:13** says,

> **When they observed the boldness of Peter and John and realized that they were uneducated and untrained men, they were amazed and recognized that they had been with Jesus (NKJV).**

Is your heart cry that you may know Christ more and more and that you would leave others recognizing you have been with Jesus? There was a boldness about Peter and John and many of disciples. It was undeniable they were operating in the power and authority of God. In verses **19-20**, they go on to say,

> **Peter and John answered them, "Whether it's right in the sight of God for us to listen to you rather than to God, you decide; for we are unable to stop speaking about what we have seen and heard" (NKJV).**

They couldn't stop talking about Jesus!

May God gift us with the boldness and passion to speak about the Kingdom of God and labor in the harvest fields because of all we have seen, heard, and experienced! How can you boldly labor in the harvest fields for Him TODAY?

How can you make Monumental Moments and live to multiply His movement today?

DAY 34: DON'T MAKE THE SAME MISTAKE AGAIN

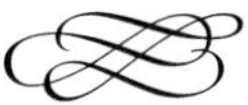

As I reread **Genesis 3** and take a closer look at the fall of man through sin and disobedience to God, my heart desires all the more to honor God and stay far from sin. Here is the deal. We all have sinned. **Romans 3:23** clearly explains that. Even as children of God that have experienced salvation through Jesus Christ, we still continue to sin. Hopefully, the longer we walk with Christ, the less we see unintentional or even intentional sin as we are made more and more into His image.

Sin left undealt with can lead us down a very dangerous, slippery slope. Do you ever intentionally pause to pray and ask God to search your heart? Do you ask Him to reveal sin or sinful areas in your life?

I have noticed how acts of sin can quickly become a habit if left swept under the rug, unacknowledged, or unconfessed before God. If we are not careful, it can get easier every time we sin, and before we know it, we can be bound to a sinful pattern. It can feel less alarming or even less repulsive the more we engage in sin. Sin may even become a new normal or even a comfortable standard if not addressed.

God, in His loving nature, does not want to leave us where we are. His desire is that we grow in Him, turn from sin, and live life abundantly! He is faithful and here to help us! **1 Corinthians 10:13** says,

> **No temptation has overtaken you that is not common to man. God is faithful, and He will not let you be tempted beyond your ability, but with the temptation He will also provide the way of escape, that you may be able to endure it.**

Isn't that a beautiful testimony. God will not let us be tempted beyond our ability, but with every temptation He provides a way of escape. He helps us. I can think of a perfect example where God helped mankind who had fallen into temptation and sin. It goes right back to the garden with Adam and Eve, where it all began!

Please read **Genesis 3:22-24** with me,

> **Then the Lord God said, "Behold, the man has become like one of us in knowing good and evil. Now, lest he reach out his hand and take also of the tree of life and eat and live forever—" therefore the Lord God sent him out from the garden of Eden to work the ground from which he was taken. He drove out the man, and at the east of the garden of Eden he placed the cherubim and a flaming sword that turned every way to guard the way to the tree of life.**

There was another tree God did not want man to touch—the tree of life. This time, He drove man out of the garden, placed a cherubim on the east side of the garden and added a flaming sword that turned every way to guard the tree and keep man away.

No doubt about it, God provided additional guidance to help man not make the same type of mistake again. Are you wanting to go deeper with God? Ask God today to search your heart, reveal sin, repent of your sin, and ask for Him to help you not make the same sinful mistake again! He loves you and wants the best for you!

How can you make Monumental Moments and live to multiply His movement today?

DAY 35: KNOCK, KNOCK

Knock, knock. I know you want to say, "Who's there?" The truth is, I don't have a joke for you but another God-Story! That's the exact sound I heard at the door when I was working at the desk in my hotel room in Salt Lake City, Utah. Next thing I heard was, "Housekeeping." I thought to myself, *Well that's funny—Housekeeping just stopped by and left some fresh towels about 30 minutes ago.* Regardless, I got up and answered the door.

I was greeted by a young woman who was just as surprised as I was when I opened the door. She looked at me and said, "Oh no, no, no. I am so sorry," as she fumbled in broken English. I heard her knocking on the door, but she was knocking on the door across the hall and not my door. I smiled politely and said,

"No problem," and then I shut the door and sat back down at my computer to get back to ministry work. There was one problem though. God had other plans and other ministry for that moment! The Lord reminded me of a scripture that quickly came to mind.

> **Ask, and it will be given to you; seek, and you will find; knock, and it will be opened to you. For everyone who asks receives, and he**

who seeks finds, and to him who knocks it will be opened. Matthew 7:7-8, NIV

I had been praying for God to put another person in my path that I can share the Gospel with. I just didn't expect them to be coming to me and knocking on my door! My work was to do the work of the Father and go back into the hallway to speak with the beautiful young woman and tell her how precious and beautiful she is and how much God extravagantly loves her.

I smiled, said, "Yes Lord," prayed for the words, got up, opened the door, and politely asked for soap! Yes, I asked for soap. Don't judge! I wanted a way to reengage the conversation, and soap seemed to be the perfect segue! He did wash our sins away, right?!

She looked confused and pulled a towel off her cart. I gestured like I was washing my hands and she said in Spanish, "Oh, jabón!" We laughed together and tried saying the word for soap in each other's language. It was such a great way to engage in conversation and let our guards down as we laughed in unison. I started to talk as she pulled out her phone to utilize Google Translate—thank God for modern technology.

I told her, "Thank you." I went on to explain how beautiful she was and how precious she is to God. I told her it was not an accident she knocked on the door, and I thought it was my door and answered. I said, "God sees you. He cares so much for you and hears you." I asked how I could pray for her, and she told me she had come to America from Venezuela five months ago to get out of some hard circumstances. She also explained she had recent medical tests and biopsies. With tears in her eyes that brought tears to mine, I prayed for her and asked her if she knew Jesus who has the power to heal, save, and help us through any situation. She explained she had to get back to work, but asked if she could have my phone number to continue communicating with me and praying. Of course, I gave her my phone number! She went off to the next room and texted me immediately regarding further prayer.

God's agenda for our day is always more than we can see or

imagine! Stay alert Kingdom Laborers! May this story encourage and inspire you! Is someone knocking? Or do you have a door to knock on in the midst of your to-do list for the day? Let's stay on His Kingdom Mission. Life change is on the other side of our faithfulness, obedience, and continual "Yes" to God!

How can you make Monumental Moments and live to multiply His movement today?

DAY 36: THE BREATH OF GOD

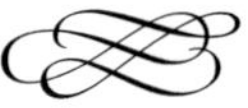

I am in an endless pursuit of more of God! I just can't get enough of Him. The more I know God, the more I desire to know Him even more. I long to be up close to Him. There is such life in His presence.

Do you remember the first time you encountered God? Did you feel joy, peace, and the fullness of life through the salvation He offers through Christ Jesus? Have you continued to seek Him and pursue an ongoing, vibrant relationship with Him? Have you been so close to God that it almost feels as though He could be breathing upon you?

I have been thinking about the scriptures throughout the Bible that describe the breath of God and the impact it has! **Genesis 2:7** says, "**And the Lord God formed man of the dust of the ground, and breathed into his nostrils the breath of life; and man became a living being" (NKJV).** Man became a living being through the very breath of God.

In the New Testament, the Bible says in **John 20:21-22,**

> **So Jesus said to them again, "Peace to you! As the Father has sent Me, I also send you." And when He had said this, He breathed on them, and said to them, "Receive the Holy Spirit" (NKJV).**

Oh to be so close to Jesus that He would breathe on us.

Job said it this way in **Job 27:3-4, "As long as my breath is in me, and the breath of God in my nostrils, My lips will not speak wickedness, Nor my tongue utter deceit" (NKJV).**

Will you commit to being a Kingdom Laborer that desires to be up close to God and positions yourself that He can continue to breathe life into you and upon you through the Holy Spirit?

Isaiah 55:6 says, **"Seek the Lord while He may be found, Call upon Him while He is near" (NKJV).**

Now is a great time to examine your own personal journey with God. Do you know Him more today than yesterday? How can you continue to grow together with Him? May your heart's cry be that you may be close enough to God that He may continue to breathe life into your soul and spirit!

As Dwight Robertson, the Founder and President of Forge, says, "The greatest gift you can give this world is your intimacy with God!"

How can you make Monumental Moments and live to multiply His movement today?

DAY 37: ARE YOU RUNNING?

Have you ever heard God whisper, ask, or say something to you in your heart? How have you responded? I must admit, there have been times I ran and immediately responded, times I have drug my feet with fear or anxiety, and times I even disobeyed and missed the moment. My heart grieves and longs to get those moments back. I know it must have grieved the heart of God too as I disobeyed.

I was challenged this week as I read about Philip and how he responded when hearing from an angel of the Lord. He arose and went immediately in response to God's request. Later in the midst of the assignment it says, "Philip ran."

Life change happened for someone because of Philip's response. Discipleship happened because Philip was a Kingdom Laborer that responded to God immediately. We read in **Acts 8** about a man of Ethiopia, a eunuch of great authority, who encountered God because a Kingdom Laborer obeyed God.

ACTS 8:26-39 SAYS,

Now an angel of the Lord spoke to Philip, saying, "Arise and go toward the south along the road which goes down from Jerusalem to Gaza." This is desert. So, he arose and went. And behold, a man of Ethiopia, a eunuch of great authority under Candace the queen of the Ethiopians, who had charge of all her treasury, and had come to Jerusalem to worship, was returning. And sitting in his chariot, he was reading Isaiah the prophet. Then the Spirit said to Philip, "Go near and overtake this chariot." So, Philip ran to him, and heard him reading the prophet Isaiah, and said,

"Do you understand what you are reading?" And he said,

"How can I, unless someone guides me?" And he asked Philip to come up and sit with him. The place in the Scripture which he read was this:

"He was led as a sheep to the slaughter; And as a lamb before its shearer is silent, So He opened not His mouth. In His humiliation His justice was taken away, And who will declare His generation? For His life is taken from the earth."

So, the eunuch answered Philip and said, "I ask you, of whom does the prophet say this, of himself or of some other man?" Then Philip opened his mouth, and beginning at this Scripture, preached Jesus to him. Now as they went down the road, they came to some water. And the eunuch said,

"See, here is water. What hinders me from being baptized?" Then Philip said,

"If you believe with all your heart, you may." And he answered and said,

"I believe that Jesus Christ is the Son of God." So, he commanded the chariot to stand still. And both Philip and the eunuch went down into the water, and he baptized him. Now when they came up out of the water, the Spirit of the Lord caught Philip away, so that the eunuch saw him no more; and he went on his way rejoicing. But Philip was found at Azotus. And passing through, he preached in all the cities till he came to Caesarea (NKJV).

Will you commit to God to respond immediately when He gives you direction from this day forward? Someone's life-changing encounter with God may be dependent on your response!

How can you make Monumental Moments and live to multiply His movement today?

DAY 38: OPEN THE EYES OF MY HEART

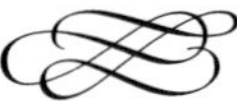

"Open the eyes of my heart, Lord. Open the eyes of my heart. I want to see You. I want to see You." Did you just read those words, or did you begin to sing them? Have you heard the "Open the Eyes of My Heart" song that Michael W. Smith released over 20 years ago?

I have found myself waking up early lately with that being my heart cry to the Lord in the mornings. I know if He opens my heart, He will change everything.

He opens the eyes of our heart to know Him more. We see it repeatedly throughout Scripture. Look at one example in **Acts 16:13-15:**

> **And on the Sabbath day we went outside the gate to the riverside, where we supposed there was a place of prayer, and we sat down and spoke to the women who had come together. One who heard us was a woman named Lydia, from the city of Thyatira, a seller of purple goods, who was a worshiper of God. The Lord opened her heart to pay attention to what was said by Paul. And after she was baptized, and her household as well, she urged us, saying, "If you**

have judged me to be faithful to the Lord, come to my house and stay." And she prevailed upon us.

Lydia was gathering with the women to pray like she had many other sabbaths before. But this sabbath was different. The Lord opened Lydia's heart to pay attention to Paul's teaching that day. She was attentive and engaged. She didn't just show up and check the box. She was moved to respond and be baptized along with her household as well. Her heart was opened, and she immediately responded personally, publicly, and walked forward in Kingdom Laborership. Something shifted that day outside the gate by the riverside. What an amazing day it must have been. Women gathered, but we hear about Lydia's story—God opened her heart and the hearts of her family members.

How can we combat routine, the mundane, and going through the motions as we walk with God? It can certainly happen, no matter how long or far we have walked with the Lord. What if we paused and asked God to open the eyes of our heart today?

Do you think He can take us deeper? Can He bring about change? Will you ask Him to open your heart today?

How can you make Monumental Moments and live to multiply His movement today?

DAY 39: VITAMIN J

I was serving as a greeter at church recently, engaging in conversation with someone after the service. We were processing the great sermon that was preached and talking about the week ahead. As the woman went to leave for the day, she walked away and said, "I had to come get my dose of vitamin J today."

I stood there rather puzzled. I had never heard someone refer to encountering Jesus as taking a vitamin, getting their daily dose of Jesus, or vitamin J.

While my friend had found a funny, creative way to refer to the church service, as I continued to process that phrase a while, I thought, *I want more of Jesus than just a daily dose. I want it all—all of Him.* I need Him every moment—not just as a pick me up, quick shot of vitamin water, or immunity shot.

I must be honest, there have been plenty of times throughout my life my actions have proved otherwise. Though I desire to live for God and pursue Him with all I am, my life does not always reflect it. It looks more like coming to Him to get a quick pick me up at times.

My heart knows, I desperately need Jesus. Do you?

There is so much more to living a life with Christ. It's more than a daily dose. The Bible says, in His presence is the fullness of joy. My heart breaks when I realize I have left Jesus waiting or that I have only briefly checked in with Him to ask for or receive something.

How often do we leave God waiting? How often is God an afterthought? How often do we just check in for a quick pick-me-up once a week?

He is worthy of so much more. He is holy and worthy of everything! He gave His life for us.

The Bible says in **John 5:39-40**, **"You search the Scriptures because you think they give you eternal life. But the Scriptures point to Me! Yet you refuse to come to Me to receive this life" (NLT).**

Are you intentionally going to Jesus praising, praying, and offering all that you have to Him? Are you continually pursuing Him?

In **John 10:10** Jesus says, **"I came that they may have life and have it abundantly!"**

Pause with me today and praise the King of Kings for all He is and everything He is worthy of. Look beyond getting a daily dose of Vitamin J, and worship The Great I Am, The Alpha and Omega, Yahweh, and Jehovah every chance you have!

How can you make Monumental Moments and live to multiply His movement today?

DAY 40: A CHIP OFF THE OLD BLOCK

We had just anchored the rickety dive boat for another mermaid-like adventure along the wall—a 7,000-foot Barrier Reef drop-off outside of Grand Turk. The engine shut off, and we could only hear waves crashing against the tiny fiberglass boat. The silence was calming. We all gathered to suit up while we were getting the important dive briefing of the underwater conditions, terrain, and sea life. Wetsuits, masks, snorkels, fins, BCD's (Buoyancy Control Devices), dive computers, and weights all piled up at our feet as we listened intently to understand what was ahead.

You have probably heard the phrase, "You had me at hello!" Well. . . the dive master had my attention at, "Chip!" That's correct, Chip. He explained, we would descend to about 80 to 90 feet, travel out against the current, and follow the wall for about 20 minutes before we headed back with the current. We may encounter sharks, and a famous one named, "Chip!"

All the island locals knew him and could point him out from all the others. He had a chip out of his fin from previous shark fights. *Great, more sharks,* I thought.

We suited up and jumped in the water. Before long we had descended to 85 feet, fought the current, and enjoyed the salty, wet panoramic views underwater through our masks. Vibrant colors of blue, green, purple, orange, and colors I can hardly describe made up the coral gardens, wall, and sea life. We were floating along enjoying scenery we had only seen in photos. Then, the Divemaster pointed off into the abyss and made the shark sign. We looked, and before our eyes was a shark. Then he made another sign as if he was cutting scissors. Somehow, we knew what he meant. It was Chip!

I watched as Chip cruised the wall as if going out for a Sunday afternoon stroll. He kept with our pace of the current and drifted effortlessly. Chip was amazing. He was so beautiful to watch. I tried to do name or word association so as to not forget him. I thought of the phrase, "Chip Off the Old Block!" The phrase is simply referring to someone who resembles a parent.

Then I thought, "I want to be a Chip Off the Old Block." No, I don't want to be a shark, and I don't want to have visible battle scars. I want to be like my Father. I want others to say I resemble my Heavenly Father.

When others see me, I want them to see my Abba Father. Is that your prayer? Do you want to be recognized as a child of God?

The Bible says in **John 1:12-13**,

But to all who did receive Him, who believed in His name, He gave the right to become children of God, who were born, not of blood nor of the will of the flesh nor of the will of man, but of God.

To be a "Chip Off the Old Block" means you imitate your father.

Ephesians 5:1-21 says,

Therefore be imitators of God, as beloved children. And walk in love, as Christ loved us and gave Himself up for us, a fragrant offering and sacrifice to God. But sexual immorality and all impurity or covetousness must not even be named among you, as is proper among saints. Let there be no filthiness nor foolish

talk nor crude joking, which are out of place, but instead let there be thanksgiving. For you may be sure of this, that everyone who is sexually immoral or impure, or who is covetous (that is, an idolater), has no inheritance in the kingdom of Christ and God. Let no one deceive you with empty words, for because of these things the wrath of God comes upon the sons of disobedience. Therefore, do not become partners with them; for at one time you were darkness, but now you are light in the Lord. Walk as children of light (for the fruit of light is found in all that is good and right and true), and try to discern what is pleasing to the Lord. Take no part in the unfruitful works of darkness, but instead expose them. For it is shameful even to speak of the things that they do in secret. But when anything is exposed by the light, it becomes visible, for anything that becomes visible is light. Therefore, it says, "Awake, O sleeper, and arise from the dead, and Christ will shine on you." Look carefully then how you walk, not as unwise but as wise, making the best use of the time, because the days are evil. Therefore, do not be foolish, but understand what the will of the Lord is. And do not get drunk with wine, for that is debauchery, but be filled with the Spirit, addressing one another in psalms and hymns and spiritual songs, singing and making melody to the Lord with your heart, giving thanks always and for everything to God the Father in the name of our Lord Jesus Christ, submitting to one another out of reverence for Christ.

How can others see the Father in you? How are you honoring Him well?

Sharks are known for being aggressive! Do you need to aggressively deal with fleshly areas in your life so others may see you representing your Heavenly Father rather than hearing stories about your own battle scars? Pray to God about it.

How can you make Monumental Moments and live to multiply His movement today?

DAY 41: DID YOU SEE THAT?

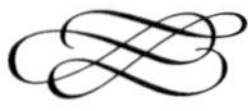

The Bible is loaded with so many incredible treasures to discover! I have been camping out for a while in **John 4**. I have been intrigued with the interactions at Jacob's well in the town of Sychar when Jesus speaks with the Samaritan woman.

Jesus has a lengthy conversation with the woman and then says, **"I who speak to you am He" (John 4:26, NKJV).** He is declaring to her that He is the Messiah. Then, right after He makes that statement, verse 27 says,

> **And at this point His disciples came, and they marveled that He talked with a woman; yet no one said, "What do You seek?" or "Why are You talking with her" (NKJV)?**

Some versions of the Bible say the disciples marveled at the interaction between Jesus and the Samaritan woman, but other versions use words like surprised, shocked, amazed, wondered, greatly amazed, greatly surprised, or astonished. The fact is, they walked up to an unusual situation—something completely out of their norm.

I can't help but wonder about the disciples who walked up to the well to see Jesus talking with this woman. They were shocked, amazed, and speechless, and no one said out loud, "What do you seek?" No one asked, "Why are you talking with her?" Given the scripture in verse **27**, I am almost certain they were thinking about those questions in their minds.

The very next verse, **John 4:28**, says, **"The woman then left her waterpot, went her way into the city . . ." (NKJV).** Did she leave in awe and wonder of what Jesus said? Did she leave because of possible facial expressions or the body language of the disciples who walked up as she was talking with Jesus as they stood surprised?

It has me asking myself, "How often am I shocked and speechless as the Lord speaks with others around me? And how do I react?" How often do I ask God, "Why . . . ?" Do I look perplexed? Or do I question the situation? Is my heart pure?

How would you respond in this situation?

I pray as Christians and God's Kingdom Laborers we are all found celebrating the work of God in everyone's life. Let's be His cheerleaders and part of the King's front-row, fan club that celebrates every single God encounter with those in front of us!

How can you make Monumental Moments and live to multiply His movement today?

DAY 42: DO YOU WANT TO BE MADE WELL?

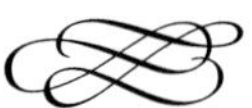

As I long to keep a surrendered posture before the Father and keep the atmosphere of revival in my heart that I have been experiencing since the Asbury Revival, I have been asking Jesus more and more to search me and reveal the weak, lame, and blind areas of my heart.

I found something interesting this week as I read a story in **John 5**.

John 5:1-9 says,

After this there was a feast of the Jews, and Jesus went up to Jerusalem. Now there is in Jerusalem by the Sheep Gate a pool, which is called in Hebrew, Bethesda, having five porches. In these lay a great multitude of sick people, blind, lame, paralyzed, waiting for the moving of the water. For an angel went down at a certain time into the pool and stirred up the water; then whoever stepped in first, after the stirring of the water, was made well of whatever disease he had. Now a certain man was there who had an infirmity thirty-eight years. When Jesus saw him lying there, and knew that he already had been in that condition a long time, He said to him, "Do you want to be made well?" The sick man answered Him,

> **"Sir, I have no man to put me into the pool when the water is stirred up; but while I am coming, another steps down before me." Jesus said to him, "Rise, take up your bed and walk." And immediately the man was made well, took up his bed, and walked (NKJV).**

This man had an infirmity for many years—thirty-eight to be exact. Jesus asked him, "**Do you want to be made well?**" The Bible says the sick man answered Him, "**Sir, I have no man to put me into the pool . . .**" Jesus responded and said, "**Rise, take up your bed and walk.**" Jesus asked the man about his desire to be made well, but the man responded—not with a yes or no, but with how it was not possible in his own strength or through the men around him. Regardless, Jesus still responded, "**Rise, take up your bed and walk.**"

I understand this story is referencing his physical limitations, but I have been considering it in the light of my own personal, spiritual limitations and heart infirmities, if you will.

I believe God is asking, "**Do you want to be made well?**" He is declaring, "**Rise, take up your bed and walk.**" His sons and daughters and the "great multitude of sick people" with wounded hearts have been waiting at the water's edge far too long.

It's time to be healed by the Great Physician. Nothing is too big for God. It's time to "**Rise, take up your bed and walk.**" Don't wait. Rise up and run for the King and His Kingdom. The harvest is plentiful!

Do you want to be made well today? Ask the Lord and He will answer!

How can you make Monumental Moments and live to multiply His movement today?

DAY 43: THE LOVE OF THE FATHER

My husband Scott and I had the privilege to travel to QwaQwa, South Africa on a mission's trip about 15 years ago. And there is a moment I still think about to this day—nearly 5,475 days later.

I was working alongside of one of the women in the village and helping to broom her dusty, red dirt floor in her modest, cinder block home. She was carrying her handsome son, Andreece, who was about 10 months old. He was tied on her back the traditional African way with bright, colorful cotton fabric.

He kept watching me contently with his captivating brown eyes as I cleaned alongside his mom. We made our way out to the small garden to handwash clothes in a washtub with water that had clearly been used for days and days. Andreece continued to smile and stay engaged as I helped his mom chore by chore.

Somewhat settling into life as a local, I asked Mom through an interrupter, "Do you mind if I hold Andreece? Will you teach me the African way to tie him on my back?" She laughed, untied Andreece from her back and moved him over to mine. She laughed again. I had to be a sight! We took a couple photos, and I continued to work by her side. Then as the hot, African sun started to set, it was a sign it was time to head back to our hotel for the evening.

As I wrapped up, the mother looked at me ever so intently and spoke something in her native clucking language of QwaQwa. I knew it was something important. She wanted me to understand to the fullest.

The interpreter began engaging in conversation directly with the mother as the mother kept looking at me with a new sense of urgency. Finally, I stepped up. "What is she saying," I asked the interpreter. The young interpreter looked with tears in her eyes and said, "She said please take my son. Take him to America for a better life."

My heart broke. I knew I could not just head back to the U.S. with a child from South Africa. And I did look to my husband for confirmation. I thought, "What mother could meet a stranger and give up her son for a chance at a new life?" What a sacrifice for a parent. Then, the Holy Spirit revealed, "I know and understand." He dropped in my spirit **John 3:16, "For God so loved the world, that He gave His only Son, that whoever believes in Him should not perish but have eternal life."**

God did that. He gave His one and only son, so you and I could have a better life—eternal life through Christ Jesus.

Consider the sacrifice and cost Christ paid for you. May we be forever grateful and mindful of the price paid on Calvary. Is there someone you are willing to have a conversation with to tell them the Good News of Jesus so they can have a new life in Christ—an eternal life in Heaven?

Don't wait! Take action today!

How can you make Monumental Moments and live to multiply His movement today?

DAY 44: RUN FOR THE ROSES

Larry Collmus announced in a captivating voice the 149th running of the Kentucky Derby at Churchill Downs in Louisville, Kentucky. He kept everyone on the edge of their seats as powerful thoroughbreds made their way to the starting gates to compete in the elite "Run for the Roses" and to have a chance to enter the Kentucky Derby's Winner's Circle.

An extravagant 1.86 million dollars of a 3-million-dollar purse was up for grabs. Spectators tuned in from around the world to hear Collmus announce this after the final turn coming into the homestretch . . . "Here's Mage coming strongly down the outside. Angel of Empire is putting on his run. And there's one furlong to run. Two Phil's on the inside trying to hold off Mage. Mage is taking the lead here as they come into the final sixteenth. And it's going to be Mage to win the Kentucky Derby!" All of this passionately announced as you hear the grandstands erupt in celebration and disappointment simultaneously.

What a race. Mage was not a favorite going into the race—in fact he was a long shot. But Mage had a great deal of determination and talent.

These 1,000-pound horses are raced to the finish line at speeds of around 37 mph by jockeys weighing less than 126 pounds (soaking wet) with all their equipment.

Jockeys aboard the horses have very little control outside of the bridle and bit the horse is wearing. They steer, hold back, coax and release the horse to run primarily through the bridle. Watching the race and seeing the bridles being put on in the paddocks, I couldn't help but think of **James 1:26, "If anyone thinks he is religious and does not bridle his tongue but deceives his heart, this person's religion is worthless."**

As Kingdom Laborers desiring to run the race, share the Gospel of Jesus Christ, and minister to others here, there, and everywhere, we should learn to bridle our tongue. We should be disciplined and in control to bring God all glory! It's so important to follow the conviction of the Holy Spirit.

Do you need to repent to God this week for anything spoken that wasn't God-honoring? Do you need to apologize or ask for forgiveness for words you spoke that did not build up? Take a moment now to ask God to forgive you, lead you, and guide you! He is waiting for you! Let's learn from our mistakes, take responsibility, and live to edify Christ in word and deed!

He is your greatest fan, believes in you, and is cheering you on!

How can you make Monumental Moments and live to multiply His movement today?

DAY 45: WHAT'S ON IN THE BACKGROUND?

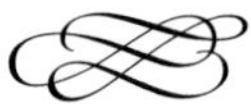

"O Lord, you have searched me and known me! You know when I sit down and when I rise up; You discern my thoughts from afar. You search out my path and my lying down and are acquainted with all my ways. Even before a word is on my tongue, behold, O Lord, you know it altogether." Psalm 139:2-4

"Search me, O God, and know my heart! Try me and know my thoughts! And see if there be any grievous way in me, and lead me in the way everlasting!" Psalm 139:23-24

"Bless the Lord, O my soul, and all that is within me, bless His holy name!" Psalm 103:1

May I share another personal story with you? I was at a Forge event recently with many of the Forge Speakers. Early in the day I was preparing for the team gathering, running errands, and filling my car with supplies. Loaded up, I began driving the car toward the facility. I had my cell phone connected to

Bluetooth through the car and was playing worship music and singing "You Are Worthy of It All" at the top of my lungs as the music vibrated the steering wheel and seats! It must have sounded like a beat box to the cars around me. I was simply having another moment with God.

I pulled up to the designated location and parked in an unloading zone to begin unpacking the vehicle. I grabbed my phone and car keys to begin making the many trips inside. Several speakers noticed my car and quickly ran to the vehicle to help unload the boxes. After it was unloaded, one of the speakers said, “Let me park the vehicle for you.” I kindly said thank you and turned over the keys.

Moments later he walked in with a puzzled look on his face and said, "What on earth were you listening to?" I said, "Worship music, why?" He said, "That absolutely was not worship music. It was blasting and full of curse words." I was floored and just as shocked as he was! That was nothing like what was playing when I left the vehicle.

I do not listen to music outside of worship, jazz and maybe a little country music from time to time. I quickly realized I had my cell phone linked to Bluetooth, so I could play worship through Spotify on the rental car. I didn't pay attention to what was on in the background before I connected, as I quickly linked my phone to the rental car and turned worship on.

I have been allowing God to teach me in the silence in the days since. The truth is, there are hidden, unexposed, and underlying sinful bents and habits that are underneath the surface of our lives that God wants to reveal loud and clear. Sometimes, he reveals it in the silence and sometimes through the noise.

When is the last time you have asked God to search your heart? May I encourage you to pause and ask God to search you and see if there are any grievous ways within you? May *all* that is within you bless His Holy Name!

How can you make Monumental Moments and live to multiply His movement today?

DAY 46: WHAT'S THE EXCUSE THIS TIME?

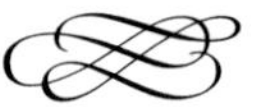

We all have different reasons or even excuses as to why we don't do things. For me, I had many excuses as to why I did not want to scuba dive with my adventure-seeking husband. I was: panic-stricken after a horrible first experience; fearful of the unknown; afraid of little to no visibility in the deep, dark waters; worried about sharks and unseen sea creatures; stressed I would do something wrong and breathe through my mask instead of my regulator; uptight that someone may kick off my mask underwater; concerned I wouldn't make it back to my children; and on and on and on.

I was overtaken with fear and with excuses. I didn't want to hear about anything I could be missing. I simply found a way to justify the fear.

How often do we as God's Kingdom Laborers let fear dictate our actions? We may choose to not step out in faith, be disobedient to Christ, willfully decide not to share the Gospel with someone or plant a seed in someone's life, all because we are crippled with fear. Fear can overshadow anything if we let it.

This recreational scuba thing may seem trivial to you. You may say, "Just don't dive, snorkel instead," or "Find another passion." I knew personally God was working on me, and He had something to teach me. I could not stay in a state of fear. If I did, it would have a grip on me. As difficult as it was, I knew I had to overcome the fear and excuses. Diving would go beyond a physical or recreational journey—it would reflect a spiritual journey with the Lord.

The Bible says in **2 Timothy 1:5-8,**

> **I am reminded of your sincere faith, a faith that dwelt first in your grandmother Lois and your mother Eunice and now, I am sure, dwells in you as well. For this reason, I remind you to fan into flame the gift of God, which is in you through the laying on of my hands, for God gave us a spirit not of fear but of power and love and self-control. Therefore, do not be ashamed of the testimony about our Lord, nor of me His prisoner, but share in suffering for the Gospel by the power of God.**

I believe we are usually always operating in either faith or fear. This scripture is a calling forth of faith—faith that has been passed down for generations. We are to fan into flame the gift of God. Fan into flame faith. Don't be crippled with fear, but operate in power, love, and self-control. Action is required! You may have to work to fan embers into flames!

Today, I call myself a scuba diver. It even sounds crazy saying it. I am a diver! I have the cards, the gear, over 50 dives logged in my dive book, nearly 40 hours underwater and qualify as a Master Diver by PADI (Professional Association of Diving Instructors) standards. I have overcome a huge fear and have fallen in love with the sport. Now, I am asking my husband to go diving. I have multiple certifications including Advanced Search and Rescue, have encountered countless sharks, dove depths up to 100 feet underwater, met new friends in the journey, and have been exposed to a new world below sea level.

God has used this newfound passion as a tool to encounter more people in recent years. God has put my feet in more airports, planes, hotels, rental car facilities, states, countries, islands, dive shops, and boat rides, introducing me to thousands more people along the way—people I can see, stop, and spend time with, and share the love of Christ. I have shared Christ with people on boats on the way to dives in the middle of the ocean and had the honor of leading a young woman to Christ at the poolside as she was folding towels.

I have learned saying "Yes" to God in faith is always worth it. He is worth it. When we say "Yes" to God and choose faith over fear, He expands our world, advances His Kingdom, encourages other people in the journey, allows us to know Him more intimately, and He creates a new level of faith and trust in our heart for Him—the one who loves us more than anything!

God is cheering you on dear Kingdom Laborer! What are you fearful of saying yes to that God may be asking of you to advance His Kingdom? Please reread **2 Timothy 1**, fan into flame faith, and walk in the fullness of all God has for you! Souls could be on the other side of your "YES!"

Romans 8:28 says, "**And we know that for those who love God all things work together for good, for those who are called according to His purpose.**"

Ask God to show you where He would love to see your "YES!" Be prepared to ditch all excuses.

How can you make Monumental Moments and live to multiply His movement today?

DAY 47: 911 EMERGENCY DISPATCH CENTER

911 is a telephone number reserved for emergency situations. In many countries around the world, 911 will get you in contact with an emergency dispatch office that has the ability to immediately send out first responders to the scene. I have been in situations where I have needed to dial 911 to get immediate help, and I know the desperation, panic, and fear that can overtake you when you feel helpless.

However, I have never been in a line of work (so I thought) where I was a first responder on the other side of a plea for help. I am starting to think a bit differently after reading **Luke 16:19-31**.

For reference, here is the scripture:

There was a rich man who was dressed in purple and fine linen and lived in luxury every day. At his gate was laid a beggar named Lazarus, covered with sores and longing to eat what fell from the rich man's table. Even the dogs came and licked his sores. The time came when the beggar died, and the angels carried him to Abraham's side. The rich man also died and was buried. In Hades,

> **where he was in torment, he looked up and saw Abraham far away, with Lazarus by his side. So he called to him, "Father Abraham, have pity on me and send Lazarus to dip the tip of his finger in water and cool my tongue, because I am in agony in this fire." But Abraham replied,**
>
> **"Son, remember that in your lifetime you received your good things, while Lazarus received bad things, but now he is comforted here and you are in agony. And besides all this, between us and you a great chasm has been set in place, so that those who want to go from here to you cannot, nor can anyone cross over from there to us." He answered,**
>
> **"Then I beg you, father, send Lazarus to my family, for I have five brothers. Let him warn them, so that they will not also come to this place of torment." Abraham replied,**
>
> **"They have Moses and the Prophets; let them listen to them."**
>
> **"No, Father Abraham," he said, "but if someone from the dead goes to them, they will repent." He said to him,**
>
> **"If they do not listen to Moses and the Prophets, they will not be convinced even if someone rises from the dead."**

The rich man is making an emergency, eternal, 911 call for help. When Abraham explained he couldn't help, the rich man says, "Then I beg you, father, send Lazarus to my family, for I have five brothers. Let him warn them, so that they will not also come to this place of torment." The rich man missed his opportunity to surrender to God, and he can't stand the thought of his loved ones being eternally in torment and separated from God like he is.

Brothers and sisters and Kingdom Laborers, you are part of a Kingdom Dispatch Office. The emergency calls are coming in. There is an emergency, and souls are on the line. You are being called to rise up and go out on assignment.

You are a Kingdom First Responder. You are here to bring the saving knowledge of Jesus Christ to the desperate, broken, and hurting that need Jesus. Eternity is at stake. Please don't delay. Take up the full armor of God (**Ephesians 6**), and Forge Forward to rescue the lost for Christ!

How will YOU respond to eternal 911 calls this week? Lives are on the line!

How can you make Monumental Moments and live to multiply His movement today?

DAY 48: WHAT'S THE TEMP?

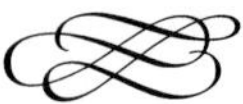

A hot tub that's not quite hot enough, an ice pack with melted ice, an oven that won't reach temp, ice tea without ice, a steam room without the steam, melted ice cream, a broken freezer full of rotten meat, a cold shower that simply won't heat up, a heating pad that will not work, an air conditioner low on coolant, a dryer with a bad heating element, an order placed for extra hot coffee that comes out lukewarm—are all things that can be frustrating. The truth is, there is a desired and "ideal" temperature to keep things perfect—either hot or cold.

Listening to my audio Bible this week left me praying through **Revelation 3** and considering the concerns with being lukewarm. I immediately was taken back to the image embedded in my heart and mind from the Asbury Revival—the words "Holiness Unto The Lord" that took center stage.

I don't know that I can describe holiness completely. When I think of holiness, I think of the Lord God Almighty, and I think of perfection. I may be at a loss for words in how to describe holiness, but I know what holiness is not. It is not living our life being lukewarm. It's not having one foot in the Kingdom and one foot in the world.

Revelation 3:14-22 says,

Write to Laodicea, to the Angel of the church. God's Yes, the Faithful and Accurate Witness, the First of God's creation, says: I know you inside and out, and find little to my liking. You're not cold, you're not hot—far better to be either cold or hot! You're stale. You're stagnant. You make me want to vomit. You brag, "I'm rich, I've got it made, I need nothing from anyone," oblivious that in fact you're a pitiful, blind beggar, threadbare and homeless. Here's what I want you to do: Buy your gold from me, gold that's been through the refiner's fire. Then you'll be rich. Buy your clothes from me, clothes designed in Heaven. You've gone around half-naked long enough. And buy medicine for your eyes from me so you can see, *really* see. The people I love, I call to account—prod and correct and guide so that they'll live at their best. Up on your feet, then! About face! Run after God! Look at me. I stand at the door. I knock. If you hear me call and open the door, I'll come right in and sit down to supper with you. Conquerors will sit alongside me at the head table, just as I, having conquered, took the place of honor at the side of my Father. That's my gift to the conquerors! Are your ears awake? Listen. Listen to the Wind Words, the Spirit blowing through the churches (MSG).

The Spirit of God is alive, moving, and blowing. The Lord calls His people to account, so they live at their best. He is calling us out of passivity, mediocracy, and complacency as He prods, corrects, and guides.

Allow God to search your heart—even the hidden, deepest, darkest places. What is your spiritual temperature? Where is He calling you further still? Make note of it and take action.

Arise, up on your feet Kingdom Laborer! About face!

Run after God. Look to God and get your marching orders and run in full surrender and obedience. He is Holy and worthy of it all!

How can you make Monumental Moments and live to multiply His movement today?

DAY 49: ALL ACCESS PASS

I was invited to a Christian concert recently by someone who helps with the promotion, touring, and production. Upon arrival, they presented me with an "ALL ACCESS" pass. Boy, did I feel important! I quickly put the ALL ACCESS badge around my neck, walked through the backstage area, then around to my seat to watch the concert. Suddenly the house lights dimmed, stage lights came on, and worship broke out, echoing throughout the packed arena.

At one point, a few songs in, people started singing in unison, "You are worthy of it all. You are worthy of it all . . ." I bowed my head in reverence, surrender, and acknowledgement of the holy moment before King Jesus. As I glanced down, the ALL ACCESS pass hanging from my neck spoke volumes—probably moreso to me personally than it did to others who saw it. The Holy Spirit was having a moment with me—another teaching moment.

I felt as though the Lord was challenging me with this: *You wear this ALL ACCESS pass around your neck, but you are not using it to the fullest in the special or restricted areas. It's just a badge. You simply have it like a piece of jewelry that you can talk about. You have it ready to grab a quick selfie for a social media highlight reel. My people have the ultimate*

ALL ACCESS pass to me since the veil was torn through the work on the cross, but it is sometimes just a badge they carry and do not use.

I was immediately reminded of **Matthew 27:50-53,**

> **And Jesus cried out again with a loud voice and yielded up His spirit. Then, behold, the veil of the temple was torn in two from top to bottom; and the earth quaked, and the rocks were split, and the graves were opened; and many bodies of the saints who had fallen asleep were raised; and coming out of the graves after His resurrection, they went into the holy city and appeared to many.**

The veil was torn on Good Friday over 2,000 years ago as Christ died on the cross. Let's pause and recognize the sacrifice Christ made, His resurrecting power, and the immediate and full access we now have with the Father because of the price Christ Jesus paid.

Let's not just wear a "Christian" badge, use it as a token, or save it for a selfie. He paid the ultimate price for us. Let's take full liberty and authority to go into the Holy of Holies with the Lord today. How will you approach God today?

How can you make Monumental Moments and live to multiply His movement today?

DAY 50: A CHRISTMAS WONDERLAND

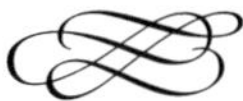

All of the twinkling lights and sparkling holiday decorations at Christmas always compete to grab my attention. There is so much to take in as you drive city streets or back country roads or walk inside of stores or throughout malls. As I enjoy all the sights of Christmas around the holiday season every year, with my various travels, I have been captivated watching children with their sweet sense of awe and wonder! No matter where I seem to travel, children appear to be truly fascinated as they experience things for the very first time.

Have you seen the wide-eyed wonder of a child as they see their first decorated Christmas tree, open a gift for the first time, taste their first Christmas cookie, or watch a holiday parade pass by on Main Street? There is pure excitement you can see in their eyes, hear in their squeals, and experience as they point and jump for joy!

It has me wondering at times, do I keep that same excitement and awe with God? We are children of God! **John 1:12-13** says,

> **But to all who did receive Him, who believed in His name, He gave the right to become children of God, who were born, not of blood nor of the will of the flesh nor of the will of man, but of God.**

Have you allowed things to become mundane with God? It does not happen overnight, but somehow one day we can wake up with a sense of casualness. It's amazing to find ourselves amidst a loving, tender, and familiar God—familiar in the sense that we truly know Him. But, have we taken Him for granted and become casual in our pursuit of Him?

As a child of God, how would you describe your time with the Father in recent days, weeks, or months? Are you awestruck and captivated with wonder and amazement? Are you expectant to learn and see new things and go deeper in your understanding of Him? Is your heart tender toward Him, or have you become lackadaisical?

Perhaps it's time we ask God for a fresh, new perspective of Him and His Kingdom. Allow Him to show you new treasures in His Word as you read the Bible and watch the miracle of Christ come alive in your heart in a new way not just during Christmas, but throughout the year!

How can you make Monumental Moments and live to multiply His movement today?

DAY 51: HOLY, HOLY, HOLY

Have you ever used the word *holy* in a phrase or sentence referring to something other than His holiness? It can happen often and easily slide off the tongue without even having a second thought. Sayings like holy smokes, holy cow, holy macaroni, and holy moley can be heard nearly everywhere these days. I have definitely used terms like that before without even thinking about it.

The truth is, the Lord is the only one worthy of being called holy. Have you paused to think of His holiness lately? I believe we can sometimes begin to take God casually the longer we journey with Him.

Let's take time to reflect on His holiness. We do not have to wait until Easter and Holy Week come around annually. We can choose to be intentional daily and acknowledge the Lord as the Holy One of Israel.

Look what the Bible says about the Lord and His holiness . . .

- **"No one is holy like the Lord! There is no one besides you; there is no Rock like our God." 1 Samuel 2:2, NIV**

- **"Give to the Lord the glory He deserves! Bring your offering and come into His presence. Worship the Lord in all His holy splendor." 1 Chronicles 16:29, NLT**

- **"Who will not fear You, Lord, and glorify Your name? For You alone are holy." Revelation 15:4, NLT**

- **"All nations will come and worship before You, for Your righteous deeds have been revealed." Revelation 15:4, NLT**

- **"Day after day and night after night they keep on saying, 'Holy, holy, holy is the Lord God, the Almighty—the one who always was, who is, and who is still to come.'" Revelation 4:8, NLT**

- **"I will show how holy My great name is—the name on which you brought shame among the nations. And when I reveal My holiness through you before their very eyes, says the Sovereign Lord, then the nations will know that I am the Lord." Ezekiel 36:23, NLT**

Oh, that we would be Kingdom Laborers that recognize His holiness and cry, "**Holy, Holy, Holy is the Lord God Almighty.**" Take a moment and pray to the Lord. How can you acknowledge the Holy One today? He is worthy of your praise and adoration. Honor Him now for all that He is to you.

How can you make Monumental Moments and live to multiply His movement today?

DAY 52: WHEN TWO WORLDS COLLIDE

As a Kingdom Laborer in God's harvest fields, I have been intrigued with the scripture about Mary and Martha that we find in **Luke 10**. To be absolutely honest, I have flat out wrestled with it at times.

We most likely all know the story where Martha graciously welcomed Jesus in her home and was excited to fix a meal for Him and the guests. We may also know the second half of the story where Mary, Martha's sister, chose to sit at Jesus' feet and learn what He was teaching rather than help Martha prepare the meal in the kitchen.

Please take a moment and read **Luke 10:38-42.**

As Jesus and the disciples continued on their way to Jerusalem, they came to a certain village where a woman named Martha welcomed Him into her home. Her sister, Mary, sat at the Lord's feet, listening to what He taught. But Martha was distracted by the big dinner she was preparing. She came to Jesus and said, "Lord, doesn't it seem unfair to You that my sister just sits here while I do all the work? Tell her to come and help me." But the Lord said to her,

> **"My dear Martha, you are worried and upset over all these details! There is only one thing worth being concerned about. Mary has discovered it, and it will not be taken away from her" (NLT).**

Are we to simply sit at Jesus' feet and not worry about serving Him? I wrestle with this because my heart is to serve Him by serving others. So, what should that look like? I know serving and working for the Kingdom is not at the expense of time alone with God. Does one take priority over the other? Can we do both and do them both well?

It can feel like a battle in this crazy busy world we live in. But, if we back up and read the start of the same chapter, we see Jesus was sending out the disciples in pairs, and these were His instructions, **"The harvest is great, but the workers are few. So, pray to the Lord who is in charge of the harvest; ask Him to send more workers into His fields" (Matthew 9:37-38, NLT).**

So, the disciples were being sent out by Jesus to encourage more workers in His harvest fields. Later in the same chapter, **Luke 10:41-42**, we find Martha, a worker who is actively working and serving, being told by Jesus,

> **My dear Martha, you are worried and upset over all these details! There is only one thing worth being concerned about. Mary has discovered it, and it will not be taken away from her (NLT).**

What is a Kingdom worker to do? I believe it's God's heart for the two worlds to collide! I believe He desires us to be in love with Him, keep our gaze on Him, and operate as a Kingdom Laborer out of the overflow of our time with Him. Jesus modeled Kingdom Laborership and selfless servanthood, and He set the standard for seeking the Father.

I witnessed the miraculous power of the two worlds colliding recently. Honestly, in the past, I can pinpoint both Martha moments and Mary moments. But recently, I had a beautiful Mary and Martha moment simultaneously as the two worlds collided. I was operating in the fullness of the gifts God has given me serving others in His harvest field while remaining in the overflow of my time with Him in recent hours, days, and weeks. My eyes stayed firmly on Him and the "why" behind Kingdom Laborership.

As we are Laborers for King Jesus in His harvest fields, let's keep our eyes fixed on the Author and Perfecter of Our Faith, be concerned with what He is concerned with, and make sure we are serving after we have spent time at His feet. We can limit the distractions like Martha encountered in the midst of serving as we recognize His presence and that He is the honored guest!

How can these two worlds collide for you this week as you labor for the King and sit at His feet?

How can you make Monumental Moments and live to multiply His movement today?

DAY 53: NO BAND-AIDS REQUIRED

I remember as a child running around the farm, riding my bike on the long, gravel farmhouse driveway, climbing the pasture fences, chasing newborn puppies, kittens, and foals, and jumping on and off of farm equipment regularly. It was all part of growing up on a horse farm in the Midwest.

I also remember my father doing everything possible to prevent me from falling on my knees as a child to avoid bumps, scrapes, bruises, and the need for princess and Elmo Band-Aids. There were times, despite his best efforts, that I would fall, scrape my knees, and cry uncontrollably. He was quick to remind me how he had warned me not to run and that I was going to get hurt if I fell. He rarely had sympathy, because he could see it coming and tried his best to warn me in advance.

Did you ever have those warnings from your parents growing up as a child? Or, if you are a parent, have you pleaded with your children to be careful so they wouldn't get hurt?

Interestingly, now as an adult and child of God, I am realizing the importance of running even faster to my Heavenly Father and falling on my knees before Him where no Band-Aids are required and where the tears are holy tears.

Luke 22:40-41 says,

> **And when He came to the place, He said to them, "Pray that you may not enter into temptation." And He withdrew from them about a stone's throw, and knelt down and prayed, saying, "Father, if you are willing, remove this cup from Me. Nevertheless, not My will, but Yours, be done."**

As Christians and followers of Christ, how often are we found kneeling physically before the Father? Has it been a while since you have pulled away from the crowds and got alone with Him? When is the last time you declared, "Nevertheless, not my will, but Yours be done," as you have sat in His presence?

The Lord waits patiently for us. Perhaps it's time to run back to the Father and fall on your knees in reverence. You can never be on your knees in prayer and praise too often before the Almighty God.

Will you allow God the opportunity to speak to you as you kneel at His feet today?

How can you make Monumental Moments and live to multiply His movement today?

DAY 54: FILL IN THE BLANK

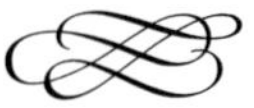

Let's play fill in the blank. "**Renew a right _______ in me.**" What was your answer?

As followers of Christ and Kingdom Laborers, we must spend time in that secret place with the Lord. Not because we have to, but because we get to. He is worthy.

We need to create space for renewal and allow Him full access and authority to renew a right "SPIRIT" within us. All too often, we go through life running full-throttle and take very little time to sit in His presence. I like to say, if we do not operate out of the overflow, it will be our undertow.

Take hold of what **Psalm 51:1-12** says:

Have mercy on me, O God according to Your steadfast love; according to Your abundant mercy blot out my transgressions. Wash me thoroughly from my iniquity and cleanse me from my sin! For I know my transgressions, and my sin is ever before me. Against You, You only, have I sinned and done what is evil in Your sight, so that You may be justified in Your words and blameless in Your judgment. Behold, I was brought forth in iniquity, and in sin

did my mother conceive me. Behold, You delight in truth in the inward being, and You teach me wisdom in the secret heart. Purge me with hyssop, and I shall be clean; wash me, and I shall be whiter than snow. Let me hear joy and gladness; let the bones that You have broken rejoice. Hide Your face from my sins and blot out all my iniquities. Create in me a clean heart, O God, and renew a right spirit within me. Cast me not away from Your presence and take not Your Holy Spirit from me. Restore to me the joy of Your salvation and uphold me with a willing spirit.

Oh, how the Lord delights in truth in the inward being and teaches wisdom in the secret heart. May He have the full authority to do His perfect work in us and renew a right spirit in each of us.

Please pause and pray with me. *Heavenly Father search me, try me, and know the innermost places. Take full control as I surrender the deepest areas of my life and heart. Allow revival and renewal in You to overtake every area of my life in Jesus' name!*

How can you make Monumental Moments and live to multiply His movement today?

DAY 55: FAMISHED

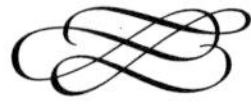

When asked to describe my trip to Asbury University where I joined thousands of others to worship God at the Asbury Revival, I found it hard to articulate and put earthly words to something so heavenly.

It made me think of the Lord's Prayer, in **Matthew 6:9-10** when it says, "**Pray then like this: 'Our Father in heaven, hallowed be Your name. Your kingdom come, Your will be done, on earth as it is in heaven.**"

Surrounded by so many hungry hearts seeking Jesus together from around the world, it felt like His Kingdom and His will on earth as it operates in heaven—at least as far as I can humanly imagine. Tender hearts were beyond hungry. They were famished for more of Jesus.

It was all about Jesus, and nothing else. Suddenly, so many scriptures were coming to life.

As I lost all track of time, 13 hours of worship felt like 10 minutes with a 1,000-year download from the Holy Spirit. Time stood still and nothing mattered but Jesus. Suddenly I thought of **2 Peter 3:8**, "**But do not overlook this one fact, beloved, that with the Lord one day is as a thousand years, and a thousand years as one day.**" Notice that

Scripture says, "**with the Lord.**" The Lord was ever so present. It was tangible, and time seemed to stand still in His presence.

My heart felt like it was exposed in the deepest most vulnerable places before the Lord and as if it went through a meat tenderizer being transformed in the most merciful hands.

Revival, renewal, revolution, and/or awakening—whatever term you choose, it all leads to a deep stirring and hunger in the soul. God is up to something around the globe! Hungry hearts are being passionately set ablaze for King Jesus.

We have seen a fresh, new outpouring of His Holy Spirit, not just at Asbury University, but on college campuses, in churches, in prayer meetings, and in gatherings around the world as thousands of famished hearts travel great distances to join others to worship, pray, surrender, repent, give their lives to Jesus, and even be baptized. There was even the movie, *Jesus Revolution,* that released at the box office shortly after the Asbury Revival. How about that for divine timing?

Behold, He is doing a new thing as it says in **Isaiah 43:19**, "**Behold, I am doing a new thing; now it springs forth, do you not perceive it? I will make a way in the wilderness and rivers in the desert.**"

Don't miss the moment! God shows no partiality as we read in **Acts 10:34**. And He gives the Spirit without measure as the Bible tells us in **John 3:34**.

Take hold of Kingdom things and help King Jesus advance His mission!

How can you lean into the King today and further His Kingdom?

Have a seeking heart for Him on earth as in Heaven. As we read in **Matthew 5:6, "Blessed are those that hunger and thirst for righteousness, for they shall be filled" (NKJV).**

How can you make Monumental Moments and live to multiply His movement today?

DAY 56: A HEART THE SIZE OF TEXAS

I have heard people say, "They have a heart the size of Texas!" In other words, they are describing someone as having a huge heart. Another way to say it is, "They are big-hearted!"

A story title recently grabbed my attention. I took the bait and clicked on the online article titled, "The Blue Whale's Heart: You Won't Believe How Huge It Really Is." I read on and quickly found myself thinking, *Now that's a heart the size of Texas!*

So intrigued, I read on and began researching other educational blogs from many other sources including National Geographic. I am not a whale expert, but I loved getting to the heart of the matter and learning new things about this massive mammal!

My heart was captivated with the facts surrounding the blue whale's heart. The details were fascinating. These mammals are the largest on earth and the size of their heart reflects it.

These creatures can grow to nearly 100 feet long and have hearts that weigh approximately 400 pounds. Knowing that the human heart weighs only approximately 10 ounces, the whale's heart is nearly 640 times larger than a human's.

There have been many articles published about these massive creatures after scientist discovered several blue whales that washed ashore in Newfoundland, Canada in 2014. They died after being stranded in thick ice off the island's coast.

Researchers took advantage of the rare opportunity to study the huge carcasses and organs. In one of the specimens, they removed the heart and preserved it using a plastination process to prevent decay.

This whale's heart has been compared to the size of a Volkswagen Beetle car! Maybe you too are thinking to yourself, *That is a heart the size of Texas!*

Upon its preservation in 2017, the heart was promptly displayed in the "Out of the Depths" art exhibit in the Royal Ontario Museum in Canada as the first and only real preserved blue whale heart in the world. Nearly one-quarter of a million people were drawn to tour the unique exhibit.

It's been said, the blue whale's heart is so large and powerful each heartbeat can be heard from over 2 miles away underwater. The heart pumps an estimated 58 gallons of blood per heartbeat.

Yes, the size and weight are hard to comprehend, but imagine hearing heartbeats from over 2 miles away! I thought about that for a moment . . . these mammals can hear each other's heartbeat for miles!

I want my heartbeat for Christ to be heard for miles! I want others to hear my heart and know who it beats for! How about you? When others hear you speak, do they hear your heart?

Luke 6:45 says,

> **The good person out of the good treasure of his heart produces good, and the evil person out of his evil treasure produces evil, for out of the abundance of the heart his mouth speaks.**

What is your heart echoing these days? People may not be able to hear your very heartbeat, but they can hear your heart as you speak.

Proverbs 4:23 says, "**Keep your heart with all vigilance, for from it flow the springs of life.**"

The Lord is looking at the state of your heart as we are reminded in **1 Samuel 16:7**, "**For the Lord sees not as man sees:**

man looks on the outward appearance, but the Lord looks on the heart."

Perhaps it is time we schedule an appointment with the Great Physician and allow Him to do heart surgery, so our heart beats for what His beats for!

Matthew 24:12 warns us about signs we will see at the end of the age, ". . . **And because lawlessness will be increased, the love of many will grow cold."**

Let's guard against frozen hearts and spiritual cardiac arrest, and live with a heart on fire and life on purpose for Jesus!

How can you make Monumental Moments and live to multiple His movement today?

DAY 57: SEEING RED

Did you ever think of yourself as God's special valentine? I am sure many of us haven't taken the time to truly process that.

You are fiercely loved by God!

When Valentine's Day rolls around every year, we celebrate it all week long at our home. If it were up to me, we would celebrate it all year long! I do try!

Know this, God sees you as His precious valentine every single day! You do not have to wait for an official holiday to be recognized as a child He loves and adores.

Statistics prove, in recent years, people have spent over 25 billion dollars on Valentine's Day, purchasing sweet treats, heartfelt gifts, mini getaways and vacations, and making reservations for special dinners with loved ones.

As you know, during Valentine's week the color red is everywhere! You can find red flowers, pillows, cards, balloons, kitchen towels, socks, candles, signs, and even special edition stamps.

Red is known to evoke many emotions. The color red is most associated with love, but it is also frequently associated with anger and aggression as well.

Regardless of what Valentine's week or even Sweetest Day holds for you every year, may you sense the lavishing love of the Father every single day.

John 15:11-13 says,

I have told you this so that My joy may be in you and that your joy may be complete. My command is this: Love each other as I have loved you. Greater love has no one than this, that he lay down his life for his friends (NIV).

God wrote *you* the longest, greatest love letter that you can cherish forever through His precious Word—the Bible. Are you reading it as a letter written for you and taking in all that He has for you?

I recently purchased the red-letter edition of the book, *The Greatest Words Ever Spoken.* It's simply a compilation of everything Jesus ever said in the Bible. Scripture after scripture directly from Jesus Himself. I have found the letters in red to simply be one continually beautiful reminder of Christ's unfailing love.

May you pause and reflect His incredible, beautiful, and sacrificial love for *you*. Take a moment, pick up His Word, and search out several scriptures in red this week. Allow the Lover of Your Soul to speak directly to *you*, His forever Valentine!

How can you make Monumental Moments and live to multiply His movement today?

DAY 58: WILL YOU?

I read this familiar passage from the Gospel of **John 4:4-15** recently and stopped two words into Jesus' question with, "Will you . . . ?" Suddenly, I was the one being asked, "Will YOU . . . ?" That's a convicting question within itself, isn't it?

> **Now [Jesus] had to go through Samaria. So He came to a town in Samaria called Sychar, near the plot of ground Jacob had given to his son Joseph. Jacob's well was there, and Jesus, tired as He was from the journey, sat down by the well. It was about noon. When a Samaritan woman came to draw water, Jesus said to her, "Will you give me a drink?" (His disciples had gone into the town to buy food.) The Samaritan woman said to Him,**
>
> **"You are a Jew and I am a Samaritan woman. How can You ask me for a drink?" (For Jews do not associate with Samaritans.) Jesus answered her,**
>
> **"If you knew the gift of God and who it is that asks you for a drink, you would have asked Him and He would have given you living water."**
>
> **"Sir"' the woman said, "you have nothing to draw with and the well is deep. Where can you get this living water? Are You greater**

than our father Jacob, who gave us the well and drank from it himself, as did also his sons and his livestock?" Jesus answered,

"Everyone who drinks this water will be thirsty again, but whoever drinks the water I give them will never thirst. Indeed, the water I give them will become in them a spring of water welling up to eternal life." The woman said to Him,

"Sir, give me this water so that I won't get thirsty and have to keep coming here to draw water" (NIV).

Jesus has always been good at asking questions. Throughout the Scriptures as Jesus taught, He had many thought-provoking questions for those He encountered. He often found a way to dig deep within, piercing the heart with His direct inquiries.

Has the Holy Spirit asked anything of you recently? Have you taken the time to process and answer Him?

In this scripture, the Lord took a physical need, engaged in conversation, asked a question, and was ready to teach profound spiritual truths in the midst of it.

It is good for us to not only read the stories within the Scriptures, but to take time to study them and allow God to examine our hearts in the process.

Take a moment today and listen carefully if God is asking YOU to do something. Will you? The question can often go far beyond the physical impact and usually has eternal significance!

Ask the Lord what He is asking of *you* these days. Be careful to listen and faithfully obey! Once He speaks to you and gives revelation, you have an increased level of responsibility.

Will you pause and seek Him now?

How can you make Monumental Moments and live to multiply His movement today?

DAY 59: WAIT . . .

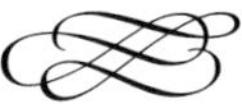

"Out of the depths I cry to you, Lord; Lord, hear my voice. Let Your ears be attentive to my cry for mercy. If You, Lord, kept a record of sins, Lord, who could stand? But with You there is forgiveness, so that we can, with reverence, serve You. I wait for the Lord, my whole being waits, and in His Word I put my hope. I wait for the Lord more than watchmen wait for the morning, more than watchmen wait for the morning. Israel, put your hope in the Lord, for with the Lord is unfailing love and with Him is full redemption. He Himself will redeem Israel from all their sins." Psalm 130:1-8, NIV

The Message version shares this same passage from **Psalm 130:1-8** this way:

Help, God—I've hit rock bottom! Master, hear my cry for help! Listen hard! Open your ears! Listen to my cries for mercy. If You, God, kept records on wrongdoings, who would stand a chance? As it turns out, forgiveness is Your habit, and that's why

> **You're worshiped. I pray to God—my life a prayer—and wait for what He'll say and do. My life's on the line before God, my Lord, waiting and watching till morning, waiting and watching till morning. O Israel, wait and watch for God—with God's arrival comes love, with God's arrival comes generous redemption. No doubt about it—He'll redeem Israel, buy back Israel from captivity to sin.**

In **Psalm 130**, the author is pleading with their whole being, waiting on the Lord.

In this fast-paced, drive-through world, it can be very difficult to wait for answers. It can be hard to "**Be still and know that He is God" (Psalm 46:10).**

Nowadays we want answers quickly, so we can move on to the next new thing. Often, we can put expectations on the Lord and in some ways demand that He works on our timeframe. We can find ourselves frustrated and even angry if we feel God hasn't met our personal timeline. We can disregard that He is God, in control, and His timing is perfect. He always has something to teach us in the waiting.

In the waiting we can either grow frustrated or we can choose to seek Him even more desperately.

Have you ever found yourself waiting on God? While you wait, are you waiting with your whole being and putting your hope in Him? Are you waiting for the Lord more than watchmen wait for the morning?

Be encouraged! "**Put your hope in the Lord, for with the Lord is unfailing love, and with Him is full redemption**," as promised in **Psalm 130:7 (NIV)**!

Stay expectant and hopeful! He is unfailing!

How can you make Monumental Moments and live to multiply His movement today?

DAY 60: ANOTHER NO-SHOW

Our town has an incredible performing arts center that offers amazing, high-quality performances. We have seen many memorable performances there. I always love getting their catalogues loaded with the scheduled shows for the upcoming months. I often have a hard time narrowing down and choosing one or two to see. Shows like *Annie* or *Sound of Music* always tug at my heartstrings.

Recently, there was a light-hearted Christian comedy musical that caught my eye. It appeared to get rave reviews. The performances would be held in the historic Schoolhouse Theater a block away from their main performing arts center—a beautiful building I have always wanted to see a performance in. It's an iconic schoolhouse on Main Street that is over 100 years old. It has a rich history. Nowadays, it hosts performances, seminars, and celebrations and is a beautiful backdrop for family photos and proposals.

I couldn't resist. I checked the calendar. There were front row seats left to the performance on the Saturday night we had available. I bought the tickets, received the email confirmation, and put it on my calendar. The event would be about four months out. My heart grew in anticipation every time I drove down Main Street and passed the schoolhouse.

The clock just keeps ticking and doesn't stop. As you know, the days are long, and the years are short! Days continue to be filled with so many important to-do's and at the same time, many opportunities. Like you, we have loved ones and families to care for, relationships to tend to, neighbors to help, jobs to complete, finances to oversee, doctors to visit, meals to make, cars to fix, animals to feed, and on and on. Life seems to have a consistently fast pace.

Fast forward a few months. With the schedule we keep, it's rare we have down time. We had been running a sprint pace for several weeks straight. When one Friday evening rolled around, my husband asked me, "What's on tap this weekend?"

"Nothing," I quickly replied. "I just want to stay home, maybe make a pot of soup, and possibly install the new front door that has been sitting in our garage for months!" I didn't even look at the calendar. I just needed space to rest and breathe!

We had an amazing weekend. I did make the soup, we turned on a college football game in the background and worked on installing our new front door. Saturday came and went. Sunday morning, we went to a worship service and continued to enjoy our Sabbath. Monday morning came quickly, and it was back to sprinting through the day. When mid-week hit, I had a thought, *When is the show? I know it's coming up soon. I can't wait to see it.*

I was too busy to check. The day kept moving, and I did too—full speed ahead. Around 3 a.m., I couldn't sleep, and I thought about the show for some reason. I searched my calendar for the date of the show. It was Saturday. Not the coming Saturday, but last Saturday—the day we chose to do nothing except stay home, make soup, and install the door. We were no-shows. We missed the show!

I was devastated. Not only did we miss the show, we wasted the tickets, threw away money, and lost the opportunity to visit the Schoolhouse Theater. My heart hurt. It was a costly weekend.

I prayed and talked to God about my disappointment and apologized for not stewarding that well. It was a moment I can never get back. I thought, *I have never been a no-show.* As I continued to think about it throughout the day, my heart grew more and more burdened.

Something was off. With a new revelation, I knew what it was. I *have* been a no-show before—many times. Unfortunately, it has been with God. There have been times, over and over, I have left Him waiting while I was busy with other things or just wanted down time.

Isaiah 30:15-18 says,

> **For thus said the Lord God, the Holy One of Israel, "In returning and rest you shall be saved; in quietness and in trust shall be your strength." But you were unwilling, and you said,**
>
> **"No! We will flee upon horses"; therefore you shall flee away; and, "We will ride upon swift steeds"; therefore your pursuers shall be swift. A thousand shall flee at the threat of one; at the threat of five you shall flee, till you are left like a flagstaff on the top of a mountain, like a signal on a hill. Therefore the Lord waits to be gracious to you, and therefore He exalts Himself to show mercy to you. For the Lord is a God of justice; blessed are all those who wait for Him.**

I love that this scripture reminds us in returning and rest we will be saved, and that quietness and trust will be our strength. It says the Lord waits to be gracious to us. He exalts Himself to show mercy to us. He is a good and loving Father.

I wonder, why are there times I leave Him waiting? Why do I not show up to be with Him and to seek Him? There is a front row seat waiting. Have you left God waiting?

The show must go on! Will you put action items in place to help you safeguard from missing precious moments with God? He deserves for us to be present. May we live our lives to show up for God and never be a no-show!

Take time to connect with God! Set up a date day with Him! Add it to your calendar, and don't be a no-show like me!

How can you make Monumental Moments and live to multiply His movement today?

DAY 61: DID YOU ALREADY PRAY THAT?

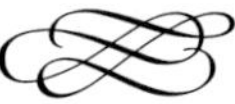

Sometimes it feels as though my prayers to the Lord are on repeat or even autopilot. It almost even seems like a version of Groundhog Day, where the prayers are monotonously repeating. Do you ever find yourself thinking, *I have already prayed about this multiple times?* At times, we can even begin to get selfishly frustrated with the Lord because He is not answering our prayers on our timeline.

Remember, the Lord longs to be in continual communication with each of us! Your prayers are an act of worship unto Him. Our creator isn't rolling His eyes and thinking, *This again, really?* No, He is lovingly waiting for another opportunity to communicate with you.

Look at Anna in the Bible who night and day with fasting and prayer was found continually worshiping God. Anna inspires me. I am sure there had to be some prayers, concerns, and conversations of Anna's that made it on repeat a couple of times as she relentlessly pursued God both night and day. I know the Lord must have been pleased to hear from her continually.

The Bible says in **Luke 2:36-38**,

> **And there was a prophetess, Anna, the daughter of Phanuel, of the tribe of Asher. She was advanced in years, having lived with her husband seven years from when she was a virgin, and then as a widow until she was eighty-four. She did not depart from the temple, worshiping with fasting and prayer night and day. And coming up at that very hour she began to give thanks to God and to speak of him to all who were waiting for the redemption of Jerusalem.**

What can we learn from the prophetess, Anna? How can we as children of God lean into the Lord and worship Him through our ongoing personal prayers? Anna didn't leave the temple. She relentlessly pursued God. She was found worshiping with fasting and prayer night and day. What a notably honorable commitment.

Sometimes I can get distracted just a few minutes into my prayer with God. Imagine the intensity of Anna's prayer life. Her fasting and prayer night and day in the temple is referred to as worship.

Will you pray with me today and ask God, "How can I honor You through continual worship and prayer? Teach me to pray and praise You continually."

Let's be found children of the Most-High God who are not ashamed to pursue Him over and over again, day and night. Don't grow weary, worship!

How can you make Monumental Moments and live to multiply His movement today?

DAY 62: MY FAVORITE THINGS

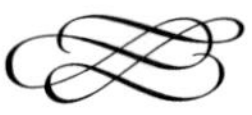

"Bright copper kettles and warm woolen mittens, brown paper packages tied up with strings, these are a few of my favorite things." As you kept reading, did you begin to find yourself humming or singing?

Can you picture Julie Andrews, who played the part of Maria, singing that song in the classic musical, *The Sound of Music?* For many of us, the moving storyline, incredible music, and beautifully breathtaking scenery of Salzburg, Austria links *The Sound of Music* book, movie, and even the musical to many fond childhood memories. When you hear the song, "My Favorite Things," it's hard to not think of *The Sound of Music.*

This week I have been questioning, "What are my favorite things?" Sparkle. It's toward the top of my list and is my favorite color! I believe it's in God's color wheel!

Many things can be at the top of our favorite things list, keeping our eyes even somewhat off of the main thing. I wonder, "Is there anything in my life, or your life that competes for God's attention?" I love what the Word of God shows us in **Hebrews 11:24-27.**

> **It was by faith that Moses, when he grew up, refused to be called the son of Pharaoh's daughter. He chose to share the oppression of God's people instead of enjoying the fleeting pleasures of sin. He thought it was better to suffer for the sake of Christ than to own the treasures of Egypt, for he was looking ahead to his great reward. It was by faith that Moses left the land of Egypt, not fearing the king's anger. He kept right on going because he kept his eyes on the one who is invisible (NLT).**

Sometimes, it can be hard to keep our eyes on The One who is invisible, when so many flashy, favorite things are everywhere. I want to keep my eyes fixed on Jesus! Do you? We know it is possible!

Hebrews 12:1-2 says,

> **And let us run with endurance the race God has set before us. We do this by keeping our eyes on Jesus, the champion who initiates and perfects our faith. Because of the joy awaiting Him, He endured the cross, disregarding its shame. Now He is seated in the place of honor beside God's throne (NLT).**

Let's be intentional to run with endurance the race God set before us by keeping our eyes on Jesus! May He be at the top of our Favorite Things list! How will you keep your eyes on Jesus this week?

How can you make Monumental Moments and live to multiply His movement today?

DAY 63: CHOOSE YOUR BATTLES WISELY

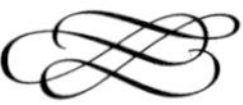

Did your mother ever tell you, "Choose your battles wisely?" In other words, you can't fight every battle, so choose the battles that are important to engage and the battles you should sit out very carefully!

Another crazy work week was quickly approaching. My husband asked me months prior to put a particular week on my calendar to travel with him and work remote because he was going to be gone several long weeks in a row. Initially, I was excited about the invitation and another opportunity to travel with him and work in a sunny destination during the winter. Just feeling the warm sun through the hotel window is a great way to help energize you!

The months quickly passed, and the flight was scheduled for 9 a.m. the next morning. Looking at my calendar and what felt like an insurmountable workload, I was trying to renege on my promise.

Reluctantly, I packed my bags at 11 p.m. the night before. Then, as the airport driver entered the driveway, I thought again about staying behind. This was unusual for me. I was trying to discern if it was me, my overwhelming schedule, the enemy, or the Lord trying to get my attention. I prayed and did not feel there was direction to stay at home other than potential comfortability of my home routine.

After about a two-hour flight, I landed in TX with my husband. He took off running immediately—racing to meetings. I stayed back at the airport for another four or five hours. I found an empty and quiet gate and continued to work on some very pressing work matters. I finally felt as though I had a brief window to grab a ride to the hotel about 20 minutes away so I could finish working at the hotel.

I pulled out my phone and scheduled a Lyft. The driver pulled up as expected, and I hopped in the car. The driver asked, "So, what are you in town for?" Then he asked what I did for a living. I explained I was traveling in with my husband for the week and that I work in ministry.

Well . . . that was all he needed to hear. He proceeded to share with me his life's concerns and tell me about his painful, recent divorce after 20 years of marriage to his high school sweetheart. He was broken. Life was hard and his heart was heavy.

I listened intently and told him I would pray for him. After asking about his faith, I encouraged him to read his Bible and get plugged back into a church and Bible-centered community. He went on to say sometimes he doesn't feel welcome in the church anymore, now that he is divorced. I continued to encourage him and share the love of Jesus with Him.

For the next 10 minutes, as we made it the final few miles to my destination, we talked, and he said, "You have no idea what this conversation meant to me today. I know you were sent by God. I wasn't even going to work and drive for Lyft today." He said, "It was not an accident that you were my first Lyft of the day. Please never stop sharing about God. I needed to hear what you had to say today. Please promise me you will continue to help others as you share about Jesus."

This man just needed to know God sees him and loves him. I simply had the opportunity to be a Kingdom Laborer for the King as the Lord ordered my steps.

I got out of the vehicle when we landed at my destination, and I smiled to the Lord and thought, *I almost didn't travel to Texas this week. I almost stayed within the comforts of my home.* It made me think of a time in the Bible when kings go out to battle.

2 Samuel 11:1-5 says,

> **It happened in the spring of the year, at the time when kings go out to battle, that David sent Joab and his servants with him, and all Israel; and they destroyed the people of Ammon and besieged Rabbah. But David remained at Jerusalem. Then it happened one evening that David arose from his bed and walked on the roof of the king's house. And from the roof he saw a woman bathing, and the woman was very beautiful to behold. So David sent and inquired about the woman. And someone said, "Is this not Bathsheba, the daughter of Eliam, the wife of Uriah the Hittite?" Then David sent messengers, and took her; and she came to him, and he lay with her, for she was cleansed from her impurity; and she returned to her house. And the woman conceived; so she sent and told David, and said,**
>
> **"I am with child" (NKJV).**

David was the King. At this time, in the spring of the year, David should have been out to battle with the kings, but instead he sent his team and army out to battle while he stayed back. There, while comfortably sitting at home, when he should have been out in the battle . . . he fell into sin and temptation.

As a Kingdom Laborer, how can you pray and remain sensitive to the Holy Spirit? Allow God to guide your steps throughout every day! Be comfortable and confidant in who you are in God, but don't get comfortable in your mission or lazy in engaging Laborership opportunities! Royal Kings and Queens, will you engage in His Kingdom battle?

How can you make Monumental Moments and live to multiply His movement today?

DAY 64: RAINWATER FROM HEAVEN

On a recent sailing trip, our adventurous hearts went hopping from island to island in the midst of the West Indies, doing our best to learn how to sail.

Daily we found ourselves kissed with a constant sea breeze, rocked to sleep by rolling waves, and dripping with salty sea water. It was amazing. In addition, day after day we were soaked by massive rainstorms that brought heavy rains, large ocean swells, and reminders of God's promises from the most extravagant rainbows—double rainbows, full rainbows, and even 360-degree rainbows. It was hard to take in all the beauty of God's creation around Grenada.

Seeing the first rainstorm approaching upon the horizon on day one had my heart anxious and heavy—nearly as heavy as my rain-soaked clothing. I didn't want to have our first adventure at the helm stamped with stormy resistance. There were already enough challenges for a sailor's maiden voyage without factoring storms into the equation.

Nevertheless, we sailed straight into the first storm. We stayed in control of the boat and the storm was gone almost as quickly as it came. I found myself reminding God it would be great to have a tropical sailing vacation without rain! Then, as quick as I could get out my request, I remembered a scripture in **Deuteronomy 11:10-17**:

> **For the land that you are entering to take possession of it is not like the land of Egypt, from which you have come, where you sowed your seed and irrigated it, like a garden of vegetables. But the land that you are going over to possess is a land of hills and valleys, which drinks water by the rain from heaven, a land that the Lord your God cares for. The eyes of the Lord your God are always upon it, from the beginning of the year to the end of the year. And if you will indeed obey my commandments that I command you today, to love the Lord your God, and to serve Him with all your heart and with all your soul, He will give the rain for your land in its season, the early rain and the later rain, that you may gather in your grain and your wine and your oil. And He will give grass in your fields for your livestock, and you shall eat and be full. Take care lest your heart be deceived, and you turn aside and serve other gods and worship them; then the anger of the Lord will be kindled against you, and He will shut up the heavens, so that there will be no rain, and the land will yield no fruit, and you will perish quickly off the good land that the Lord is giving you.**

What if I began to view storms differently? What if I recognized rain as provision from heaven—regardless of how forceful it feels or quickly it can come?

Though they can feel turbulent, storms provide the rain from heaven for God's land. They are a tangible reminder of His provision. Though we don't always see clearly through storms at the time, storms bring provision, growth, and fruit!

What storms are you facing today? Will you begin to look at them differently? Can you be thankful for the rain from heaven?

May this year bring forth fruit as God continues to faithfully provide! Be alert and expectant!

How can you make Monumental Moments and live to multiply His movement today?

DAY 65: BIG BLOCK LETTERS

"What's God going to say to my questions? I'm braced for the worst. I'll climb to the lookout tower and scan the horizon. I'll wait to see what God says, how He'll answer my complaint. And then God answered: 'Write this. Write what you see. Write it out in big block letters so that it can be read on the run. This vision-message is a witness pointing to what's coming. It aches for the coming—it can hardly wait! And it doesn't lie. If it seems slow in coming, wait. It's on its way. It will come right on time.'" Habakkuk 2:1-3, MSG

Every year in January everyone embarks on a new year! The clock does not stop. The ball drops in Times Square at midnight and a new year is underway. It's a time for many to hit reset. People are dreaming, planning, setting goals, and New Year's resolutions! In addition, many take time to pray, fast, and seek God for direction for the coming year. Then, often mid-way through the year, people take time to evaluate their progress and see if any course correction is required to continue to stay focused and on track.

Regardless of the time of year, it's always great to lean in and ask God questions! He never gets tired of hearing from you.

What questions are you asking God these days? Are you climbing, looking, scanning the horizon, and waiting with anticipation for God to meet with you and answer?

Dream big and pray bold prayers. The King is able to do far more than all we can ask or think according to the power at work in us, as we are assured in **Ephesians 3:20**!

As you dream, pray, and seek God, write down what He is speaking to you! He will make the vision clear. Be patient and wait. You may not have all the answers, but all you need is the first step! He will reveal His messages to you at the right time. Write it out boldly so you can read it on the run! As you are running the race and accomplishing His dreams for you, you will want a memory stone to remind you of His goodness and faithfulness. Keep the vision before you!

Let's be Kingdom Laborers on mission and run the race well that is set before us!

How can you make Monumental Moments and live to multiply His movement today?

DAY 66: HONEY, YOUR LIFE IS A VACATION

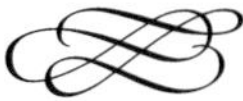

Every year when the holidays roll around and extra vacations and family time hit our calendars, we seem to be surrounded with a few extra baked goods and sugary sweet treats! You do not have to look far to find them. There is always another party or excuse to indulge. Though I would like to think that simply happens once a year, I know we have a bit of a bigger problem at our house.

My husband loves candy, anything sweet, sour, and extra sugary—nothing with chocolate, but everything Sour Patch! Whenever we are on vacation, the moment we step foot in the airport he has to find the closest store to buy a bag of Sour Patch something! Then, he will come sit next to me in the hard, industrial airport chairs and smile and say, "What? I'm on vacation!" I will sweetly remind him,

"Honey, your life is a vacation!" That's not the reality, especially when he has to live with me. But, he loves sweet treats and finding ways to justify eating sugary, sour candy.

I found myself thinking more about my statement to him, "Honey, your life is a vacation!" We can live our life in a mindset that justifies our actions. What am I doing these days? Am I telling God, "What? I'm on vacation!" In other words, I will be disciplined, focused, or engaged later.

All sweet treats and sugar aside, what point of view have you established in your mind and life for eternal Kingdom work? Are you living on mission for God or living on vacation? Do you have Kingdom goals you are working toward? What do you dream of accomplishing for the King and His Kingdom? Don't be tempted to slack. Stay focused and on mission! Learn to enjoy the sweet journey along the way as you live to bless God and advance His Kingdom!

> **God has set His throne in Heaven; He rules over us all. He's the King! So bless God, you angels, ready and able to fly at His bidding, quick to hear and do what He says. Bless God, all you armies of angels, alert to respond to whatever He wills. Bless God, all creatures, wherever you are—everything and everyone made by God. And you, O my soul, bless God. Psalm 103:19-22, MSG**

How can you make Monumental Moments and live to multiply His movement today?

DAY 67: WHERE'S WILSON?

You may be familiar with the movie, *Cast Away*. Released in 2000, it is a movie where lead actor Tom Hanks (who played Chuck Noland, a Fed-Ex executive) ends up washing ashore on a deserted island after a plane crash over the Pacific. He must learn how to survive on the island alone for years. He ends up making a handmade friend—a beloved volleyball named, Wilson! Wilson helped Chuck through a lonely season of life as he coped with being alone on a deserted island day after day.

Most of us may never know what it feels like to be alone on a deserted island for years, but loneliness in general is becoming more and more of a concern.

Though *Cast Away* was a fictitious movie, statistics say one in three Americans today feel lonely. According to a recent article published by the American Psychiatric Association (APA), the U.S. Surgeon General declared loneliness a public health epidemic in 2023. A study released in 2024 by APA found 30% of adults say they have experienced feelings of loneliness at least once per week, while another staggering 10% of people say they are lonely every day.

In addition, the findings go on to say 30% of Americans ages 18-34 say they were lonely as often as every day or several times a week.

We understand these are startling statistics and valid concerns. Thank God for medical staff that continue to help patients with their emotional wellbeing and physical health when intervention is required.

Though statistics can feel overwhelming, loneliness is nothing new. There is a common theme throughout the Old Testament and New Testament when God speaks to His people. He often assures them that though they feel alone, He is with them.

Let's remind ourselves we are not alone. The Lord is with us! Join me in reading these promises over your life!

Know this . . . The Lord is with YOU!

- Abraham
  - **"After these things the word of the Lord came to Abram in a vision: 'Fear not, Abram, I am your shield; your reward shall be very great.'" Genesis 15:1**
- Jacob
  - **"Behold, I am with you and will keep you wherever you go, and will bring you back to this land. For I will not leave you until I have done what I have promised you." Genesis 28:15**
  - **"Then the Lord said to Jacob, 'Return to the land of your fathers and to your kindred, and I will be with you.'" Genesis 31:3**
- Moses
  - **"He said, 'But I will be with you, and this shall be the sign for you, that I have sent you: when you have brought the people out of Egypt, you shall serve God on this mountain.'" Exodus 3:12**
- Joshua
  - **"No man shall be able to stand before you all the days of your life. Just as I was with Moses, so I will be with you. I will not leave you or forsake you." Joshua 1:15**

- Gideon
    - **"And the Lord said to him, 'But I will be with you, and you shall strike the Midianites as one man.'" Judges 6:16**
- Jeremiah
    - **"They will fight against you, but they shall not prevail against you, for I am with you, declares the Lord, to deliver you." Jeremiah 1:19**
- Nehemiah
    - **"And a letter to Asaph, the keeper of the king's forest, that he may give me timber to make beams for the gates of the fortress of the temple, and for the wall of the city, and for the house that I shall occupy. And the king granted me what I asked, for the good hand of my God was upon me." Nehemiah 2:8**
- Isaiah
    - **"Fear not, for I am with you; be not dismayed, for I am your God . . . " Isaiah 41:10**
    - **"When you pass through the waters, I will be with you; and through the rivers, they shall not overwhelm you; when you walk through fire you shall not be burned, and the flame shall not consume you." Isaiah 43:2**
- David
    - **"Even though I walk through the valley of the shadow of death, I will fear no evil, for You are with me; Your rod and Your staff, they comfort me." Psalm 23:2**
- Solomon
    - **"Then David said to Solomon his son, 'Be strong and courageous and do it. Do not be afraid and do not be dismayed, for the Lord God, even my God, is with you. He will not leave you or forsake you,**

until all the work for the service of the house of the Lord is finished.'" 1 Chronicles 28:20

- Jesus' Disciples
    - **"And they went out and preached everywhere, while the Lord worked with them and confirmed the message by accompanying signs." Mark 16:20**
- Early Christians
    - **"And the hand of the Lord was with them, and a great number who believed turned to the Lord." Acts 11:21**
- All of Us Forever
    - **"Teaching them to observe all that I have commanded you. And behold, I am with you always, to the end of the age." Matthew 28:20**

God is faithful and our ever-present help in time of need! Keep your eyes fixed on Jesus! He is with you! Which scripture above spoke to you? Write it out and memorize it!

How can you make Monumental Moments and live to multiply His movement today?

DAY 68: SATURATED

I spent precious time with an old friend enjoying the white, sandy beaches of Destin, Florida. She finally took the plunge and moved from Michigan to Florida to chase the sun. It was a great little getaway for me to go visit her in the Sunshine State. In the early morning hours, I decided to get in a brisk walk before the beaches filled with people. As I walked miles upon miles along the beautiful oceanside with the Lord, I had a revelation as gentle and even somewhat abrasive as the very sand I walked upon.

The further I was from the water, the less stable the ground was beneath my feet. It left me floundering with every unstable step upon the sinking sand. However, the closer I walked to the water's edge, the firmer the ground became. It was saturated with the salty seawater.

I couldn't help but think about the ground continually saturated by the constant refreshing and refining waves that provided a firm foundation to walk upon. It was such a beautiful reminder of the strength we have when we are saturated with the Holy Spirit. When we are dry and weary, we can easily crumble and stumble. But as we sit with God, we become refreshed, renewed, and stronger. I thanked the Lord for His faithfulness and continued revelations and went on to think about it more and more throughout the coming days as I vacationed with my friend.

Then, like the Lord has a way of doing, He cemented it through Scripture as I read the Word. My devotional reading highlighted **Proverbs 12:3** that says, **"You can't find firm footing in a swamp, but life rooted in God stands firm" (MSG).**

The sand I encountered in the water easily moved and shifted under my feet. The dry sand away from the water easily crumbled. But the sand on the water's edge that was exposed to all the elements and continually refined by the consistent washing of the waves provided a firm and stable footing that took me miles and miles up and down the coast!

What foundation are you standing on today? Lean into God, and ask Him how you can live rooted in Him and stand on His solid, firm foundation!

I am praying we allow God to continually renew us over and over with His powerful and refining presence that brings strength and keeps us rooted in His firm foundation.

How can you make Monumental Moments and live to multiply His movement today?

DAY 69: REBELLION

The Lord speaks to His people! How amazing is it that the God of the universe loves us so much that He chooses and desires to communicate with us individually. It may not be what we want to hear or what we are hoping for at times, but it is always what is best. He loves to be in dialogue with His children.

John 10:27 says, "**My sheep hear My voice, and I know them, and they follow Me.**"

Hearing, listening, following, and obeying are all very different disciplines. Just because we hear something, doesn't necessarily mean we are tuning in and listening or understanding. Beyond that, when we do listen, we don't always follow and obey the commands. Humans can have a way of being hard-hearted, self-centered, and a bit rebellious at times. I am guilty.

This scripture challenges me. God's sheep hear His voice. Do I always follow God when I hear and recognize His voice, or am I quick to make excuses of why I am not walking in all that He has called me to? Am I trying to justify rebellious actions? It's definitely something we all should evaluate.

I pray that we are sons and daughters of God that seek, hear, listen, and follow the commands of the Father without rebuttal or delay.

Let's take note of the scripture in **Hebrews 3:7-9,**

> **Therefore, as the Holy Spirit says, "Today, if you hear His voice, do not harden your hearts as in the rebellion, on the day of testing in the wilderness, where your fathers put me to the test and saw my works for forty years."**

It's clear, throughout Scripture and even today, men and women put God to the test. When we hear His voice, let's not test Him. May our hearts be soft and receptive, and ready to respond.

Let's trust the King in His goodness and rest in His faithfulness. **Jeremiah 29:11** says, "**For I know the plans I have for you, declares the Lord, plans for welfare and not for evil, to give you a future and a hope.**"

I am praying you choose to follow the Lord and obey His voice every day, everywhere—not just when it's convenient for you or when you like what He has to say.

What is God speaking to you? Are you obeying and following? If not, why?

Sometimes I find it vital to pause and ask God, "Is there anything you have told me or are trying to tell me that I am being disobedient in?" Take a moment now, and ask God that very question.

How can you make Monumental Moments and live to multiply His movement today?

DAY 70: DO YOU NEED NEW SHOES?

How many miles are on your shoes?

I had the privilege to attend a life-changing Life on Purpose Conference in Denver. At one point during the conference, the speaker, Dwight Robertson, said, "Your feet will take you to places others will never go." As he said that, my mind instantly started thinking about my shoes. Perhaps it's a girl thing! I wondered what condition my Kingdom shoes are in.

Shoes are a critical part of the success of an athlete. According to Runners World, the life expectancy of running shoes is not measured in months or years, but in miles. The average running shoe is made to withstand 300 to 500 miles before it begins breaking down and causing potential injury.

I see athletes all around me continually breaking in new shoes due to the distances they are traveling and miles they are quickly completing.

I kept thinking about my physical and spiritual shoes. How many miles have I completed working toward spreading the Gospel? Are my shoes collecting dust, or am I ready to take on the next pair because of the miles I have logged?

It's not a secret the Bible references feet on many occasions. For example:

- **"Ponder the path of your feet and let all your ways be established." Proverbs 4:26, NKJV**

- **"And how shall they preach unless they are sent? As it is written: 'How beautiful are the feet of those who preach the Gospel of peace, who bring glad tidings of good things!'" Romans 10:15, NKJV**

- **"Your word is a lamp to my feet and a light to my path." Psalm 119:105, NKJV**

- **"Stand therefore, having girded your waist with truth, having put on the breastplate of righteousness, and having shod your feet with the preparation of the Gospel of peace; above all, taking the shield of faith with which you will be able to quench all the fiery darts of the wicked one." Ephesians 6:14-16, NKJV**

- **"Uphold my steps in Your paths, that my footsteps may not slip." Psalm 17:5, NKJV**

In addition to feet, the Bible talks about going and sending, which require our feet to be moving! **Mark 16:15** says, **"And He said to them, 'Go into all the world and preach the Gospel to every creature'" (NKJV).**

And in **Matthew 9:37-38** it says,

> **Then He said to His disciples, "The harvest truly is plentiful, but the laborers are few. Therefore, pray the Lord of the harvest to send out laborers into His harvest."**

Are you putting constant and consistent miles on your Kingdom shoes, or is it time to dust them off and start adding more miles for the King?

How can you make Monumental Moments and live to multiply His movement today?

DAY 71: PASSPORT STAMPS

In preparing to travel oversees to share the Gospel on another mission trip, I pulled out my passport to verify the document would not expire within 6 months of my travel and that I had enough empty pages in my passport book. Good thing I checked! Not only was it about to expire, but it was also down to the last couple blank pages. Nowadays government offices recommend you have six blank pages in your passport when traveling internationally. It was time for a new passport!

As I am sure you know, an official government issued passport is your ticket into foreign countries as it validates your identity and nationality. It allows you to travel internationally and re-enter your home country! It's a document that is required for all international travel!

I have accumulated a few filled passports through the years. Stamps from all over the world fill the pages of my little blue, United States of America Passport books. It's fun to look at the books and reflect on the various journeys—globetrotting, as some would say.

But there is more to it. Regardless of the destination, I remember names, faces, and stories from nearly every trip as I have had opportunities to share Christ with others all along the way—though not every trip was an *intentional* mission trip. Some are the names of those I physically spoke with, and others are the faces of people that I missed or willfully disobeyed sharing Christ out of fear, exhaustion, lack of time, or any other excuse I could think of at the time. I missed the mark. I received the passport stamp, but missed opportunities to share Christ with those right in front of me.

Jesus had a few words to say about travel. **Mark 16:14-20** says,

> **Later he appeared to the eleven themselves as they were reclining at the table. He rebuked their unbelief and hardness of heart, because they did not believe those who saw Him after He had risen. Then He said to them, "Go into all the world and preach the Gospel to all creation. Whoever believes and is baptized will be saved, but whoever does not believe will be condemned. And these signs will accompany those who believe: In My name they will drive out demons; they will speak in new tongues; they will pick up snakes; if they should drink anything deadly, it will not harm them; they will lay hands on the sick, and they will get well." So the Lord Jesus, after speaking to them, was taken up into heaven and sat down at the right hand of God. And they went out and preached everywhere, while the Lord worked with them and confirmed the word by the accompanying signs.**

Jesus said, "**Go into all the world!**" But . . . there is an "And!" We are to "***GO* into *ALL* the world, *AND PREACH the Gospel* to ALL creation!**"

Though it is wonderful when we get opportunities to share the Gospel abroad, we don't need a physical passport or to jump on an airplane to go and preach the Gospel to all of creation. There are opportunities within your office, neighborhood, grocery store, library, gym, laundromat, sports league, car dealership, art gallery, airport, etc., etc.—every place the Lord takes you! Look for opportunities.

Aside from passport stamps, as you look to get punches on your local loyalty cards, ask the Lord to put people in your path. Live to share the Gospel with all creation wherever you go! I love how **Mark 16:20** says the disciples "**went out and preached *everywhere* while the Lord worked with them and confirmed the Word by the accompanying signs!**"

Let's GO Kingdom Laborers, AND PREACH the Gospel. Tell others what Christ has done for you, how He has changed your life, and what He can do for them! Where will you go today? Will you commit to tell others about Christ?

How can you make Monumental Moments and live to multiply His movement today?

DAY 72: AUTOPILOT

I love hearing how God is working in the lives of others. It is always a source of encouragement. We have so much to learn from one another.

I asked a friend recently, what is God speaking to you these days? She shared a small piece of her huge heart with me, and here is what she explained . . .

In **Psalm 51:12**, David asked God: "**Restore to me the joy of your salvation.**" She went on to say it's as if David at some point lost his joy, or his relationship with God had become stale.

She tenderly shared with me that she too has been praying this scripture as she found herself feeling mundane and sometimes going through the motions in her relationship with Jesus. She said the joy she once had in the Lord has waned. If we are truly honest, we know that can happen. There have been times in my walk with the Lord that I too have coasted or been on autopilot.

We all can experience this in relationships. For example, the same electricity we once felt with our spouse may no long have the same spark. We get "used to" that person and maybe begin to take them for granted when they don't delight us in the ways they had in the past.

We have to guard against this. The enemy would love nothing

more than to keep you there in the middle of complacency as you walk with God.

There is good news. We have a loving Father to run to. We can always ask God to restore to us this amazing joy! He is the author and creator of joy, and He wants us to experience IMMEASUREABLE joy in our relationship with Him! There is certainly NO END to the delightful qualities of God!

She is absolutely right! This challenged me to also ask the Lord to restore joy in areas where I have hit *autopilot* in my walk with Him.

Will you take a moment to pray to God today, and ask Him to reveal Himself to you in a new, fresh, and exciting way? Ask Him to spark newfound joy for Him within your heart? He would love to honor that request!

Let's collectively, as Kingdom Laborers, pray **Psalm 51:12** over ourselves and our loved ones. Ask God to restore the JOY of His salvation! May we learn to live in the overflow of His extravagant joy!

How can you make Monumental Moments and live to multiply His movement today?

DAY 73: REMEMBERING

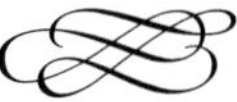

"Oh give thanks to the Lord; call upon His name; make known His deeds among the peoples! Sing to Him, sing praises to Him; tell of all His wondrous works! Glory in His holy name; let the hearts of those who seek the Lord rejoice! Seek the Lord and His strength; seek His presence continually! Remember the wondrous works that He has done, His miracles, and the judgments He uttered, O offspring of Abraham, His servant, children of Jacob, His chosen ones." Psalm 105:1-6.

When our children were young, we always had music playing in the background. It was echoing throughout our home, backyard, and cars. In addition, my kids were all taking music lessons and were in various music classes throughout the week. Music was a big part of our life.

Occasionally, a random praise party would break out, and we would worship at the top of our lungs and dance throughout the house. It was contagious! One by one, everyone would stop and join in the fun for a few minutes to worship and sing praises to God. Those are such fond family memories I carry.

Before long, as the kids quickly got older and their schedules were more and more demanding, the spontaneous dance and worship parties faded away. Looking back, it's as if they paused overnight. It wasn't that we were no longer thankful. It was simply that we did not take the time to express our praise and celebrate God's work like we had in the past!

Sometimes we can find ourselves so busy with daily routines that we do not take the time to stop and celebrate, rejoice, and be thankful for all God has done. We can be laser-focused and on a mission to accomplish a task, check the box, and look ahead to the next thing demanding our attention on our to-do list.

Gratitude is a discipline that needs to be continually exercised. Pausing and being thankful is very different than having intentions to pause and be thankful!

In reading this verse, I had an epiphany. It's been too long since my heart has truly given thanks to God.

When is the last time you stopped, called upon the name of the Lord, and thanked Him for all He has done for you? There are countless miracles and wondrous works He has done in your life.

This Scripture in Psalm 105 is a call for those who seek the Lord to rejoice! It's an invitation to give thanks; sing praise; glorify His Holy name; and seek Him, His strength and His presence, continually. It is a beckoning to remember the wondrous works God has done.

Will you join me in pausing to give intentional thanks to God? Let's call upon His name and tell of His amazing works. Let's sing a song of praise to the King. Glory In His name and rejoice today. He is worth celebrating.

Seek the Lord and His strength and seek His presence continually! May we not forget, but be ones who forever remember, acknowledge, and celebrate all the wondrous works and miracles He has done. We do not have to wait for a day like Thanksgiving that rolls around only once per year to share our gratitude with God!

May we not be stingy with our praise to the Glorious King of Kings! Will you freely and extravagantly share with Him today and every day your thankfulness?

How can you make Monumental Moments and live to multiply His movement today?

DAY 74: IT'S NOT ALL FUN AND GAMES

People of all ages from all over the world engage in this daily. It's available in many different languages. Recent stats say over 3 million people play it and know the clock resets every night at midnight. It's a word game that quickly became a craze. Can you guess it? It's The New York Times' game, Wordle.

Perhaps you know of it or even play too!

I was recently introduced to this addictive, 5-to-10-minute game along with millions of others. I quickly found myself striving to conquer the word of the day and counting down the time until the next day's word was released. I had ridiculous excitement and anticipation for the next game, like a child waiting for their birthday to arrive.

I watched my stats and followed my winning streak closely. I even shared my scores and stats with friends and family. When I awoke in the morning, I would be excited to think through my first 5 letter word choice to make my best attempt at guessing the day's word in less than the five tries allotted.

Then, one morning like many previous others, I grabbed my phone to play the Wordle game of the day! But, this time I quickly paused. I heard a small still voice within my spirit asking a simple, yet profound question that pierced my heart. "Are you more excited about Wordle or My Word?"

I knew that wasn't a question I would ask myself. I knew that was the Holy Spirit asking me. God is good at asking questions.

Here are a few from His Word to remind us...

- **"Then the Lord God called to the man, "'Where are you?'" Genesis 3:9, NIV**

- **"Then [Jesus] asked them, 'But who do you say I am?'" Matthew 16:15, NIV**

- **"Jesus responded, 'Why are you afraid? You have so little faith!'" Matthew 8:26, NIV**

- **"Jesus immediately reached out and grabbed him. 'You have so little faith,' Jesus said. 'Why did you doubt me?'" Matthew 14:31, NIV**

- **"After breakfast Jesus asked Simon Peter, 'Simon son of John, do you love Me more than these?'" John 21:15, NIV**

When God asks a question, He deserves a response! God is gracious, merciful, and slow to anger. In His loving kindness, He will ask us questions that search our soul to refine us and make us further into His image.

May I challenge all of us to ask God to search our heart, to be Christians quick to listen for His voice, and to be faithful followers willing to alter our actions to honor Him above all things?

Is there anything in your life that may be coming between you and the Lord or His precious Word? If the answer is yes, or if something quickly comes to mind, do your best to realign and make the necessary changes to place God at the forefront where He belongs! He is always worth it.

How can you make Monumental Moments and live to multiply His movement today?

DAY 75: TODAY'S DEPOSIT - $81,000,000,000,000

Imagine an unexpected notification coming across your phone regarding recent banking activity within your account. You pause and take a moment to sign in to your account and review the activity through your online portal. You look over your account and begin to scrutinize the transactions and see a very unusual and alarming number in the ledger with zero after zero after zero.

Maybe, at first, you would look closely to see if it was a withdrawal or deposit. Then after the initial shock, maybe you would begin to investigate to better understand what happened.

According to news segments and online articles, a bank employee discovered a sizable error in a customer's account. The bank erroneously credited a customer $81,000,000,000,000! That's right. There are 12 zeros listed. An account was credited 81 trillion dollars. The actual credit was instead supposed to be $280.

The mistake was overlooked by not one, but two employees before it was cleared to be processed in the system. The deposit posted. A third employee finally noticed the error after the payment had been processed, and the bank initiated a transaction reversal within several hours. Imagine being a multi trillionaire—at least for an hour or two!

Apparently, this was not a one-time occurrence. Reports noted the bank had 10 "near misses" in 2024 with errors that equated to at least one billion dollars worth of wrongful transactions that were eventually corrected.

This is not the first time I have heard of such a fortune and misfortune in a day! According to an article published by Newsweek, a family in Seattle discovered their bank account had a negative $99,999,999,999.22. It's one thing to see a crazy deposit, but imagine seeing an overdraft of over 99 billion dollars! With digital banking continually on the rise, errors like this will most likely be increasing exponentially.

Regardless of the number of zeros, the placement of the decimals, the negative or positive, these are earthly treasures and temporary riches. They may be here today and gone tomorrow or here one moment and gone the next in scenarios like we just read.

Though we are to steward carefully what the Lord has entrusted to our care and multiply our resources for His glory, our minds are not to be fixated on the things of this world. There are eternal riches we should keep our eyes fixed upon!

It reminds me of what the Apostle Paul shared in addressing the believers in Ephesus as he wrote Ephesians. In **Ephesians 3:7-12** we read,

> **Of this gospel I was made a minister according to the gift of God's grace, which was given me by the working of His power. To me, though I am the very least of all the saints, this grace was given, to preach to the Gentiles the unsearchable riches of Christ, and to bring to light for everyone what is the plan of the mystery hidden for ages in God, who created all things, so that through the church the manifold wisdom of God might now be made known to the rulers and authorities in the heavenly places. This was according to the eternal purpose that He has realized in Christ Jesus our Lord, in whom we have boldness and access with confidence through our faith in Him.**

There is so much to unpack here, but I want to *zero in* on one phrase today. By God's grace, Paul was to preach the *unsearchable riches of Christ*! There is an endless supply of unsearchable riches of Christ.

Honestly, sometimes I have been found guilty of spending more time reviewing my bank account than searching the treasures waiting for me in the Word of God.

What about you? Through Christ, we have an unending, infinite, boundless, limitless, eternal treasure that has no end. It's worth far more than quantifiable trillions. Do we truly understand the value and eternal wealth in the riches of Christ?

I love the prayer for spiritual strength that Paul goes on to pray a couple of verses later as he humbly submits to the Father and acknowledges the riches of His glory. Will you take a moment and pray this prayer of spiritual wealth from **Ephesians 3:14-21** over you and your loved ones?

> **For this reason I bow my knees before the Father, from whom every family in heaven and on earth is named, that according to the riches of His glory He may grant you to be strengthened with power through His Spirit in your inner being, so that Christ may dwell in your hearts through faith—that you, being rooted and grounded in love, may have strength to comprehend with all the saints what is the breadth and length and height and depth, and to know the love of Christ that surpasses knowledge, that you may be filled with all the fullness of God. Now to Him who is able to do far more abundantly than all that we ask or think, according to the power at work within us, to Him be glory in the church and in Christ Jesus throughout all generations, forever and ever. Amen.**

How can you make Monumental Moments and live to multiply His movement today?

DAY 76: IN IT TO WIN IT

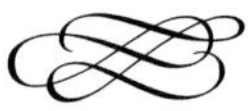

My family ran a 5K terrain race in Colorado, and it was a muddy mess! The adventurous side of me thought it could be a fun, 50th birthday present to give to my husband and another family adventure for the books.

It was our first-ever terrain race. We had no idea the mess we were about to encounter as the race began. Within the first few hundred feet, we faced our first obstacle. It was simple—run up over a mud-packed hill and back down through a pool of muddy water. We were now knee-deep in the race and the mud. This first obstacle left us running the remainder of the race in soaked socks and shoes and carrying an extra five pounds of mud on each shoe!

One of the family members, (the most girly one of the bunch), after much contemplation ran full throttle over the hill, only to run into the muddy pool of water and slide. That's right. She slid flat on her back. Hearing a scream, "Mom", I turned to see her entire body covered in mud except for her precious face. She was now all in. With mud dripping from nearly every part of her body, including her eyelashes, she got up and continued putting one foot in front of the other toward the next unforeseen obstacle. From running and hanging to climbing and crawling, she continued toward the finish line with the family. The race was hot, difficult, and full of so many unknowns at what was around every corner. But we pressed on. We were in it to have fun and finish, but not necessarily win. During the race, I couldn't help but think about Paul's words of wisdom in the Bible.

- **"Don't you realize that in a race everyone runs, but only one person gets the prize? So run to win!" 1 Corinthians 9:24, NLT**

- **"I press on to reach the end of the race and receive the heavenly prize for which God, through Christ Jesus, is calling us." Philippians 3:14, NLT**

As I ran, I kept thanking God for the journey and adventure we were on together. But, in the praising, I was praying. I prayed the Lord would teach me how to run to win and how to press on through the mess and obstacles to reach the end of the race God is calling me to.

How can you run to win? How can you press on for the heavenly prize? Lean into the Lord today, and ask for His guidance, wisdom, and perspective!

Keep running with endurance for the King! There is a prize awaiting your race.

How can you make Monumental Moments and live to multiply His movement today?

DAY 77: RIGHT TURN, LEFT TURN, OR U-TURN?

Are you a planner like I am? Do you get bent out of shape or do feathers get ruffled when plans change? I am sure you handle it better than I do! My family can help attest to that. I like to have things planned out, and I don't appreciate it when I have to alter course. Part of the problem is I try to maximize time and opportunities and fill every moment. I feel like I am missing out if something gets changed.

I have noticed through the years, God enjoys disrupting "my plans" and has a way of taking me off my course and on a route all His own. It's not always easy, but I am learning to pause and ask God to show me what He is up to! His plans always far exceed mine!

The Lord is teaching me valuable lessons through **1 Chronicles 17**. David had in his heart to build a house for the Lord, and the Ark of the Covenant. David made plans. David told his friend, Nathan, the prophet of his plans. And, that very night the Lord visited Nathan the prophet and said, "**Go and tell my servant David, 'Thus says the Lord: It is not you who will build Me a house to dwell in'" (1 Chronicles 17:4).** So, in obedience Nathan went and spoke to David explaining all the Lord had said.

David listened. He didn't kick and scream. He did not get angry and choose to go through with his plans anyway. This was a huge turn and change in David's plans.

Instead, David went and sat with the Lord. The Bible says in **1 Chronicles 17:16-20,**

> **Then King David went in and sat before the Lord and said, "Who am I, O Lord God, and what is my house, that You have brought Me thus far? And this was a small thing in Your eyes, O God. You have also spoken of Your servant's house for a great while to come, and have shown me future generations, O Lord God! And what more can David say to You for honoring Your servant? For You know Your servant. For Your servant's sake, O Lord, and according to Your own heart, You have done all this greatness, in making known all these great things. There is none like You, O Lord, and there is no God besides You, according to all that we have heard with our ears."**

When your plans change, can you simply sit with the Lord and say, **"Who am I, O Lord God?"** Can you do it with a sincere heart without being disappointed or frustrated—and simply be in awe of God for who He is?

Can you trust His ways are better and higher than yours? Let's rest in **Proverbs 19:21**: **"Many are the plans in a person's heart, but it is the Lord's purpose that prevails" (NIV).**

How can you make Monumental Moments and live to multiply His movement today?

DAY 78: SEARCHING FOR ANSWERS

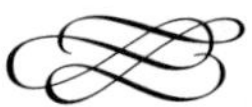

I spent some precious time alone with God at camp one summer. It was just me, my Bible, journal, and empty Adirondack chairs around me in the midst of thousands of acres of rolling hills, vibrant evergreen trees, and the picturesque backdrop of the Colorado Rocky Mountains.

I was crying out to God for help, relief, and answers regarding continued prayers I had taken to Him. I held out my cupped hands before Him as a symbol of what I was yet again carrying and bringing to Him.

During my quiet time with God, I saw an image in my mind of the Lord's hands supporting the weight of mine, as He reminded me this weight is His weight too. He doesn't want me going through this life alone. He doesn't want anyone going through life alone. He desires to be in a relationship with every one of us. I paused to thank Him and take in the moment. Then, I sensed a prompting in my heart from the Lord to turn to Psalm 32. I opened my Bible, looked up the verse and started reading. Suddenly, I stopped at **Psalm 32:8** which says, **"I will instruct you and teach you in the way you should go; I will counsel you with My eye upon you."**

As I read, **"I will instruct you and teach you in the way you**

should go; I will counsel you with My eye upon you," I knew God wouldn't fail me. I also knew I needed to be so up close and personal with Him to see Him and His eyes as He leads, instructs, teaches, and counsels me. He promises to instruct us and teach us in the way we should go. And His eyes will counsel us as He watches over us. How close are you to God these days? Do you recognize Him?

All of us are going through life searching for answers. Some don't know exactly what it is they are seeking, but are wrestling to fill a void and God-sized hole in their heart. Others are on a journey with Jesus searching and praying for wisdom and instruction.

I spent the first 27 years of my life not knowing God and searching aimlessly for answers. Now, I'm spending the remainder of my days looking to Him for direction.

Are you searching? There is great news! God Himself holds all of the answers. He promises to instruct us! Don't take your eyes off of the King! Even if you stumble or fall, get back up, and keep your eyes on Jesus!

How can you make Monumental Moments and live to multiply His movement today?

DAY 79: LUNGSFUL OF PRAISE

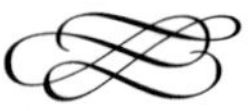

Every once in a while, I will run as part of my workout regimen. I try to run from running! The most I have ever trained for or ran was a half marathon. It was not something I would call fun. There were moments and days in training where it was hard. It was hard on my body and my lungs. There were moments it felt like I just couldn't take a deep breath, and moments where it was simply hard to breath. I had a faithful friend I trained with, and we ran a lot of miles together. She carried scripture cards with her and would read verses as we ran. She would challenge me to pray and praise while we ran even though I did not feel like it. It taught me the power of praise.

Never run out of praise! From prayers of faith, to cries for deliverance, to declarations of confidence, to a resounding lungful of praise, David in the Bible wore his heart on his sleeve before the Lord even at an old age. The Lord desires for us to share our innermost thoughts with Him. Psalm 71 is a great example of leaning into God through every emotion and sealing thoughts and emotions with heartfelt praise!

Psalm 71

I run for dear life to God,
I'll never live to regret it.
Do what You do so well:
get me out of this mess and up on my feet.
Put Your ear to the ground and listen,
give me space for salvation.
Be a guest room where I can retreat;
You said Your door was always open!
You're my salvation—my vast, granite fortress.
My God, free me from the grip of Wicked,
from the clutch of Bad and Bully.
You keep me going when times are tough—
my bedrock, God, since my childhood.
I've hung on You from the day of my birth,
the day You took me from the cradle;
I'll never run out of praise.
Many gasp in alarm when they see me,
but You take me in stride.
Just as each day brims with Your beauty,
my mouth brims with praise.
But don't turn me out to pasture when I'm old
or put me on the shelf when I can't pull my weight.
My enemies are talking behind my back,
watching for their chance to knife me.
The gossip is: "God has abandoned him.
Pounce on him now; no one will help him."
God, don't just watch from the sidelines.
Come on! Run to my side!
My accusers—make them lose face.
Those out to get me—make them look
Like idiots, while I stretch out, reaching for You,
and daily add praise to praise.
I'll write the book on Your righteousness,
talk up Your salvation all the day long,

never run out of good things to write or say.
I come in the power of the Lord God,
I post signs marking His right-of-way.
You got me when I was an unformed youth,
God, and taught me everything I know.
Now I'm telling the world Your wonders;
I'll keep at it until I'm old and gray.
God, don't walk off and leave me
until I get out the news
Of Your strong right arm to this world,
news of Your power to the world yet to come,
Your famous and righteous
ways, O God.
God, You've done it all!
Who is quite like You?
You, who made me stare trouble in the face,
Turn me around;
Now let me look life in the face.
I've been to the bottom;
Bring me up, streaming with honors;
turn to me, be tender to me,
And I'll take up the lute and thank You
to the tune of Your faithfulness, God.
I'll make music for You on a harp,
Holy One of Israel.
When I open up in song to You,
I let out lungsful of praise,
my rescued life a song.
All day long I'm chanting
about You and Your righteous ways,
While those who tried to do me in
slink off looking ashamed (MSG).

Do you make sure to never run out of praise for the Lord? Does your mouth brim with praise to Jesus who is worthy? Do you daily add praise to praise even if you do not feel like it? Do you post signs making His right-of-way? Are you telling the world of His wonders? Are you thanking Him, letting out a lungful of praise? Are you chanting about Him all day long?

Today would be a great day to start and a great day to continue to praise Jesus!

How can you make Monumental Moments and live to multiply His movement today?

DAY 80: BREAKER, BREAKER, ONE-NINE

Growing up on a horse farm in small town U.S.A. had our little world revolving around all things horses—mostly Quarter Horses, or (*hauses*) as I can still hear my dad playfully say in his Kentucky accent that moved with him to Michigan!

Dad was a horse trader and quite a good one. He and Mom raced, trained, bred, raised, and sold horses, and skillfully matched pedigrees to create champions.

My sister and I tagged along everywhere with Dad and Mom—always in the back seat of the pickup truck that was hauling a loaded-down gooseneck horse trailer filled with saddles, alfalfa, and a few horses.

We went to horse auctions where Dad was the auctioneer many Friday and Saturday nights. We went to racetracks around the country where we were the underdogs that somehow had a horse that went number one in the nation! Not bad for a man that did not have more than a seventh-grade education. He may not have been book-smart, but Dad was sure street-smart.

It felt like he knew everyone and could talk with anyone. My family was on the road a lot during my childhood, always "chasin' them horses" as Grandma would say.

That lifestyle kept our family putting many miles on Dad's Ford pickup trucks.

For some time, Dad traveled with an old-school, CB radio! CB is short for Citizens Band radio, which is a short-distance system for two-way voice communication. For some, that may feel as ancient as an 8-track tape! I remember as a kid so many times hearing "Breaker, breaker, one-nine, anyone got a copy?" Often you would lean in to hear the next conversation hitting the airways while on the roadways!

Channel 19, a.k.a. one-nine, back in the day was the most popular general channel that everyone tuned into! It was one way to kick the boredom of hours and hours of driving. Truckers wanting to start a conversation would say, "Breaker, breaker, one-nine, anyone got a copy?" This was a way to signal they wanted to interrupt the conversation, and officially announce they were going to start talking. "Anyone got a copy?" was a way to ask, "Is anyone out there listening?"

Though Channel 19 still exists on CB radios, it has become less utilized as cellphones have overtaken communication these days.

I passed a semi-truck on the road recently. I'm not quite sure why, but for a split second I had a flashback of my childhood. It was a moment where my sister and I aggressively pulled the fake ropes in the backseat of our pickup truck and arm pumped up and down to make the traditional gesture to get the truck driver in the lane next to us to honk his horn! I smiled at the memory, all the while, I could almost here, "Breaker, breaker, one-nine!" It was a glimpse back into the carefree days of my youth.

The thought of "Breaker, breaker, one-nine," left me leaning in a little closer this time now that I have a few more miles under my belt.

Suddenly, the phrase that I hadn't heard in years had me wondering, when was the last time I have called upon God—not just for an emergency, but for general conversation? I certainly never go a day without talking. But do I go a day without talking to God? Conversations with God do not have to be formal. He is always waiting and available. How often am I busy on "other channels" so to speak that I don't tune it to talk with God?

The Bible is filled with scripture about calling upon God. Here are just a few I would love to broadcast!

- **"For everyone who calls on the name of the Lord will be saved." Romans 10:13, NIV**

- **"I call upon You, for You will answer me, O God; incline Your ear to me; hear my words." Psalm 17:6**

- **"For You, O Lord, are good and forgiving, abounding in steadfast love to all who call upon You." Psalm 86:5**

- **"When he calls to me, I will answer him; I will be with him in trouble; I will rescue him and honor him." Psalm 91:15**

- **"Peter replied, "Repent and be baptized, each of you, in the name of Jesus Christ for the forgiveness of your sins, and you will receive the gift of the Holy Spirit. For the promise is for you and for your children and for all who are far off, everyone whom the Lord our God calls to Himself." Acts 2:38-39, NIV**

How are you doing with calling upon God? Has it been a while, maybe a few years, months, weeks, days, or hours? Don't wait another second!

How are you doing with listening and responding to God? Has He been trying to get your attention with a form of "Breaker, breaker, one-nine, anyone got a copy?"

In good old-fashioned CB terms, the response would be, "10-4," "Roger," or "Copy that," which simply means I hear you! Or even a "Ten-nine," meaning please repeat! You do not need a handle, call sign, or nickname to call upon God. God knows who you are and where you are! It's time to communicate with the Almighty God!

Breaker, breaker, one nine, anyone got a copy?

How can you make Monumental Moments and live to multiply His Movement today?

DAY 81: SING A NEW SONG

Music is powerful. It doesn't take us long to learn lyrics. What's the song in your heart these days?

Have you ever thought about how easy it is to get a song stuck in your head on repeat, or how you can become a creature of habit at times and just "go through the motions" and listen to something over and over?

Psalm 96:1-13 is a great reminder of how you can hit reset rather than repeat!

Worship in the Splendor of Holiness
Oh sing to the Lord a <u>new song</u>;
sing to the Lord, all the earth!
Sing to the Lord, bless His name;
tell of His salvation from day to day.
Declare His glory among the nations,
His marvelous works among all the peoples!
For great is the Lord, and greatly to be praised;
He is to be feared above all gods.
For all the gods of the peoples are worthless idols,
but the Lord made the heavens.

Splendor and majesty are before Him;
strength and beauty are in His sanctuary.
Ascribe to the Lord, O families of the peoples,
ascribe to the Lord glory and strength!
Ascribe to the Lord the glory due His name;
bring an offering, and come into His courts!
Worship the Lord in the splendor of holiness;
tremble before Him, all the earth!
Say among the nations, "The Lord reigns!
Yes, the world is established; it shall never be moved;
He will judge the peoples with equity."
Let the heavens be glad, and let the earth rejoice;
let the sea roar, and all that fills it;
let the field exult, and everything in it!
Then shall all the trees of the forest sing for joy
before the Lord, for He comes,
for He comes to judge the earth.
He will judge the world in righteousness,
and the peoples in His faithfulness.

Will you consider taking time today to write and sing a "NEW SONG" to the Lord, to bless His name? You do not have to be a singer or songwriter, and it doesn't have to be for the world to hear. It can simply be something from your heart to His—between you and the Lord.

Declare His glory and His marvelous works! He is greatly to be praised! Tell Him! Ascribe to the Lord the glory due His name! May the heavens hear the roar of your praise as you sing aloud a new song!

How can you make Monumental Moments and live to multiply His movement today?

DAY 82: ARE YOUR NOTIFICATIONS TURNED ON?

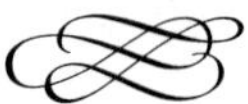

What is your screen time this week? Do you ever pay attention to screen time notifications coming across your phone weekly? Many phones send the owner notifications updating the daily average screen time—letting them know if it increased or decreased from the week prior. Vital information for those mindful of their allocated time on social media, games, productivity, finance etc.!

I received a notification last week on my phone that my screen time decreased from the week prior. It made me pause and think to myself, "What did I do differently? Has my time alone with the Lord decreased this week too?" It was as if the visual reminder helped me to question and scrutinize my engagement with the Lord for the week. I had to question, "Am I seeking first the Kingdom of God as directed in **Matthew 6:25-34**?"

> **Therefore, I tell you, do not be anxious about your life, what you will eat or what you will drink, nor about your body, what you will put on. Is not life more than food, and the body more than clothing? Look at the birds of the air: they neither sow nor reap nor gather into barns, and yet your heavenly Father feeds them.**

> **Are you not of more value than they? And which of you by being anxious can add a single hour to his span of life? And why are you anxious about clothing? Consider the lilies of the field, how they grow: they neither toil nor spin, yet I tell you, even Solomon in all his glory was not arrayed like one of these. But if God so clothes the grass of the field, which today is alive and tomorrow is thrown into the oven, will He not much more clothe you, O you of little faith? Therefore, do not be anxious, saying, "What shall we eat?" or "What shall we drink?" or "What shall we wear?" For the Gentiles seek after all these things, and your heavenly Father knows that you need them all. But seek first the Kingdom of God and His righteousness, and all these things will be added to you. Therefore, do not be anxious about tomorrow, for tomorrow will be anxious for itself. Sufficient for the day is its own trouble.**

Perhaps we can all ask ourselves, "What is my screen time this week? How does it compare to my Bible time or quiet time with the Lord? Is my Bible time up or down from last week? Am I growing and making Him a priority?"

I am praying we are! And, if you haven't been making the King a priority—start where you are! God will meet you where you are at!

How can you make Monumental Moments and live to multiply His movement today?

DAY 83: DRESSED FOR ACTION

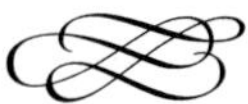

Athletes, sport enthusiasts, tradesmen, musicians, barbers, technicians, teachers, professionals—basically mankind, knows the value of investing in good equipment, gear, and tools. It can help keep you safe, up your game, make you more effective and efficient, lighten your load, make the journey more enjoyable, and ultimately serve you well in action!

My husband is an adventure-seeker and lifelong learner. It can make for a tiring combination at times for me to try and keep the pace! He is always wanting to conquer a new sport or tackle a new adventure! He is all about lifting weights, riding motocross bikes, hunting, building a home, fixing cars, scuba diving, playing an instrument, learning to sail, and jumping on the bandwagon with me occasionally to hike, play tennis, go for a bike ride or snorkel. He has no interest in simply completing a task, but rather conquering it. He has always taught me the importance of dressing appropriately for the adventure at hand and having the appropriate equipment, which makes all the difference.

In reading in **Luke 12** recently, I gained a renewed understanding for the importance of being dressed for the Father's action!

Luke 12:35-48 says,

"Stay dressed for action and keep your lamps burning, and be like men who are waiting for their master to come home from the wedding feast, so that they may open the door to him at once when he comes and knocks. Blessed are those servants whom the master finds awake when he comes. Truly, I say to you, he will dress himself for service and have them recline at table, and he will come and serve them. If he comes in the second watch, or in the third, and finds them awake, blessed are those servants! But know this, that if the master of the house had known at what hour the thief was coming, he would not have left his house to be broken into. You also must be ready, for the Son of Man is coming at an hour you do not expect." Peter said,"

"Lord, are you telling this parable for us or for all?" And the Lord said,

"Who then is the faithful and wise manager, whom his master will set over his household, to give them their portion of food at the proper time? Blessed is that servant whom his master will find so doing when he comes. Truly, I say to you, he will set him over all his possessions. But if that servant says to himself, "My master is delayed in coming," and begins to beat the male and female servants, and to eat and drink and get drunk, the master of that servant will come on a day when he does not expect him and at an hour he does not know, and will cut him in pieces and put him with the unfaithful. And that servant who knew his master's will but did not get ready or act according to his will, will receive a severe beating. But the one who did not know, and did what deserved a beating, will receive a light beating. Everyone to whom much was given, of him much will be required, and from him to whom they entrusted much, they will demand the more."

Kingdom Laborers and servants, stay dressed for Kingdom action, and keep your lamps burning! Put on the full armor of God daily, get the heavenly tools and resources you need to stay in the fight, seek first the Kingdom of God, be in the Word of God daily, saturate your life with worship of the King, surround yourself with other believers where iron sharpens iron, don't forsake fellowship within your local church body, pray to the Father continually, ask for His presence to lead and guide you, and be found dressed for action and in the action!

Are you ready? If not, what do you need to do to stay awake and alert?

How can you make Monumental Moments and live to multiply His movement today?

DAY 84: HITTING JESUS

It was Good Friday. I woke up to spend time with the Lord, but it wasn't like every other morning. I was so much more aware with hindsight and faith the fullness the day held because of the sacrifice of our Savior. I had such a tender heart for the burden He carried.

After my morning quiet time, I went to the grocery store, filled up my car with gas, and then went through the car wash—more common, everyday activities. I left the car wash, turning out onto the main road, car still dripping with water and laced with the smell of clean soap. I headed southbound and within a minute or two, I had an encounter with Jesus.

A large, white pickup truck came barreling across traffic and through the intersection and T-boned my car, inches from the driver's door. The sound of metal scraping and plastic breaking, the smell of burning tire rubber on the pavement, and an immediate sore throat from screaming, "JESUS," left me in tears. All I could do was thank the Lord that I was okay. Trying to open the driver's door and realizing I needed to climb through the backseat to get out since my door wouldn't open, gave me a further awareness of how I was protected yet again by the Lord. The gentleman who crashed into my vehicle came running to make sure I was okay and explained over and over that he didn't see me, so proceeded through the "Stop" sign. By God's grace and mercy, I was okay, and he was too.

We called the police, followed protocol, and exchanged names and phone numbers. He said, "My name is Jesús" . . . J.E.S.U.S. I said,

"JESUS . . . You are named after Jesus. Jesús what are you doing Sunday for Easter? Are you going to church"? He quickly replied,

"No." I invited him to join us for church, in which he said he would join. *(Note: He did not end up coming. Please help me continue to pray* Jesús has an encounter with JESUS!*)*

Later that evening, I thought to myself, "I hit Jesus on Good Friday." I reflected on the meaning of the day and all it represented and realized I too most likely would have been one that would have denied Jesus and/or hit Him. It drew me closer to the Savior that night and made me view things differently.

Below is **Isaiah 53:2-6** in the Message Version. Perhaps it will help us think of Jesus' sacrifice in a new way!

> **The servant grew up before God—a scrawny seedling, a scrubby plant in a parched field. There was nothing attractive about Him, nothing to cause us to take a second look. He was looked down on and passed over, a man who suffered, who knew pain firsthand. One look at Him and people turned away. We looked down on Him, thought He was scum. But the fact is, it was *our* pains He carried—*our* disfigurements, all the things wrong with *us.* We thought He brought it on Himself, that God was punishing Him for His own failures. But it was our sins that did that to Him, that ripped and tore and crushed Him—*our sins*! He took the punishment, and that made us whole. Through His bruises we get healed. We're all like sheep who've wandered off and gotten lost. We've all done our own thing, gone our own way. And God has piled all our sins, everything we've done wrong, on Him, on Him.**

Our sins did that to Him. He took the punishment. How does that make you feel? Talk to God about it.

May we always carry a heavenly awareness of His sacrifice and ALL He has done for us. His story is worth being told and retold as long as there is breath in our lungs. Keep fighting the good fight for the ONE and ONLY JESUS who sacrificed it all for you and for me! Everyone needs to hear of His Redeeming Love!

How can you make Monumental Moments and live to multiply His movement today?

DAY 85: EL ROI

Imagine living in a foreign country that does not speak your native language. You do your best to navigate life with continual broken communication with others. You try to read signs, listen intently, and pick up on occasional words, but you limit interaction with others due to the communication barrier that exists.

I had several Hispanic friends over to my home recently. They live in the U.S., but do not speak English, and I do not speak Spanish. I have always wanted to speak Spanish but have had a difficult time learning the language.

When my friends arrived at my home, we struggled to communicate with each other. Through hand signals, Google translate, and slow communication, we were able to connect in a limited capacity!

While trying to communicate, I had worship playing in the background. I had turned worship music on earlier in the morning that continued to play throughout the day! About 6 hours into my worship playlist and about 15 minutes after their arrival, the worship music suddenly switched from English to a Spanish worship set on its own that played for over three hours—until they left my home.

I stood utterly amazed. I thought . . . God sees them. He cares for them! The God who sees wanted them to know His extravagant love for them. He wanted to speak to them in their native language!

One of the names of God in the Hebrew Bible is El Roi (Hebrew: אל ראי)! It translates to, "The God who sees me," or, "The God who sees."

It is referenced in **Genesis 16** by Hagar, a woman who was on the run. Hagar was caught in a difficult situation. She was Sarai's servant. Sarai could not conceive a child with her husband Abram. Rather than wait on God, she took matters into her own hands and told Hagar, her servant, to go and be with her husband so that Sarai could then have her child. Hagar conceived.

But before Hagar even gave birth to the newborn, Sarai became jealous and treated her harshly. So much so, that Hagar fled from Sarai and ran out to the wilderness. I'm sure Hagar felt so alone, even in her own land.

Genesis 16:13 says, "**So she called the name of the Lord who spoke to her, 'You are a God of seeing,' for she said, 'Truly here I have seen Him who looks after me.'**"

Hagar recognized God as the *God of seeing.*

David further described God with his own words years later in **Psalm 139:1-4,**

> **O Lord, you have searched me and known me! You know when I sit down and when I rise up; You discern my thoughts from afar. You search out my path and my lying down and are acquainted with all my ways. Even before a word is on my tongue, behold, O Lord, You know it altogether.**

Dearest friends, El Roi is the same yesterday, today, and forever. He sees you! He searches you and knows you. He cares so much for you and desires to meet you where you are! Regardless of how you feel, you are not forsaken, abandoned, or alone.

Will you take time to acknowledge El Roi today? What would you like to talk to Him about? Share your burdens with Him. Don't run from God. Run to Him!

How can you make Monumental Moments and live to multiply His movement today?

DAY 86: THE LABORING SERVANT

God is so good to us and desires to give us wisdom and revelation. Sometimes when we know God is speaking to us, it can be overwhelming—in a good way!

Have you ever recognized the Lord was speaking to you and felt an immense weight or responsibility? I have been there. Sometimes it can take a moment to process the fullness of the gravity. Do not let it cause you to be fearful or paralyzed.

I am so intrigued with Mary's response to the angel when she found out she would conceive and bring forth a Son—Jesus. She says in **Luke 1:38**, **"Behold, I am the servant of the Lord; let it be to me according to your word."**

The road that was ahead of Mary was hard. Laboring is hard. Having unanswered questions can be hard. I don't even think Mary understood the complexity and magnitude of the task before her. But she was willing to labor and to serve regardless. There is an eternal reward when we choose to be a servant and work for the Father!

Join me in reading Mary's story in **Luke 1:26-38**:

In the sixth month the angel Gabriel was sent from God to a city of Galilee named Nazareth, to a virgin betrothed to a man whose name was Joseph, of the house of David. And the virgin's name was Mary. And he came to her and said, "Greetings, O favored one, the Lord is with you!" But she was greatly troubled at the saying, and tried to discern what sort of greeting this might be. And the angel said to her, "Do not be afraid, Mary, for you have found favor with God. And behold, you will conceive in your womb and bear a son, and you shall call his name Jesus. He will be great and will be called the Son of the Most High. And the Lord God will give to Him the throne of his father David, and He will reign over the house of Jacob forever, and of His kingdom there will be no end." And Mary said to the angel,

"How will this be, since I am a virgin?" And the angel answered her,

"The Holy Spirit will come upon you, and the power of the Most High will overshadow you; therefore the child to be born will be called holy—the Son of God. And behold, your relative Elizabeth in her old age has also conceived a son, and this is the sixth month with her who was called barren. For nothing will be impossible with God." And Mary said,

"Behold, I am the servant of the Lord; let it be to me according to your word." And the angel departed from her.

Kingdom Laborers and servants of God, may I encourage you today? Don't be afraid at what is ahead of you! Do the hard things God asks of you! The Holy Spirit is with you! The power of the Most High will overshadow you! Nothing is impossible with God!

May we position ourselves before the LORD and say, "Behold, I am the servant of the Lord." What is He asking you, His servant, to do today? Let's labor for His Kingdom cause today and every day!

How can you make Monumental Moments and live to multiply His movement today?

DAY 87: SABBATH REST

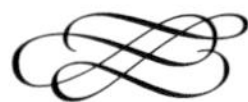

My husband is always on the go. He is so ambitious. It's one of the things I love about him. But he finds it very difficult to sit and rest. I try to keep his pace, but I find myself getting tired trying to keep up.

Rest is important to the Lord. The Lord created it for us. The word "sabbath" is mentioned 172 times in the King James Version of the Bible. A sabbath is a day of rest, a religious observance and abstinence from work. I am not always good at resting. Besides trying to keep the pace with my husband, I have dreams and goals I too have set to accomplish! Sometimes, I feel as if I don't have time to rest.

Have you ever felt that way? If it isn't the world putting pressures on us, we have a way of putting heavy weight on ourselves.

At times, we can find ourselves weary and worn out from all the demands of life. Sure, there are seasons and circumstances that can contribute to those feelings, but when we recognize our physically or spiritually weakened state, we should first look to see if we are honoring a sabbath day of rest and keeping our time with the Lord!

We can help to prevent a state of weariness by not compromising and always honoring the sabbath weekly. Choose a day and set it aside for the Lord! Trust that He will multiply your efforts the remainder of the week that you will continue to bear fruit while you rest on your sabbath!

A sabbath is so important to God that He included it as one of our Ten Commandments!

> **Remember the Sabbath day, to keep it holy. Six days you shall labor, and do all your work, but the seventh day is a Sabbath to the Lord your God. On it you shall not do any work, you, or your son, or your daughter, your male servant, or your female servant, or your livestock, or the sojourner who is within your gates. For in six days the Lord made heaven and earth, the sea, and all that is in them, and rested on the seventh day. Therefore, the Lord blessed the Sabbath day and made it holy. Exodus 20:8-11**

The Lord went on to explain it again to Moses in **Exodus 31:12-17**:

> **And the Lord said to Moses, "You are to speak to the people of Israel and say, 'Above all you shall keep my Sabbaths, for this is a sign between Me and you throughout your generations, that you may know that I, the Lord, sanctify you. You shall keep the Sabbath because it is holy for you. Everyone who profanes it shall be put to death. Whoever does any work on it, that soul shall be cut off from among his people. Six days shall work be done, but the seventh day is a Sabbath of solemn rest, holy to the Lord. Whoever does any work on the Sabbath day shall be put to death. Therefore, the people of Israel shall keep the Sabbath, observing the Sabbath throughout their generations, as a covenant forever. It is a sign forever between Me and the people of Israel that in six days the Lord made heaven and earth, and on the seventh day He rested and was refreshed" (NKJV).**

Friends, let's honor the Lord and trust Him in keeping a sabbath day of rest! The sabbath is a holy day set apart for YOU! Will you take time today and schedule your weekly sabbaths?

How can you make Monumental Moments and live to multiply His movement today?

DAY 88: NO PHONE ZONE

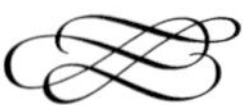

It was so great to gather with the family! Now that our children are older and are spread throughout the country, the moments we can capture together under one roof feel even more precious!

We decided to meet up together for Christmas at a tropical destination in the Caribbean to have a white Christmas—sandy style! We were there to unplug and just enjoy each other's company, the salty sea, and endless turquoise water!

One morning our baby (now a grown adult) woke up somewhat panicking. She ran her phone to us. The phone was continually beeping, vibrating, and saying, "Calling Emergency Services." Then it went to the dreaded green screen, all while continuing to beep and vibrate. There was no response on the touch screen. Being international, we tried to think creatively. We opened our laptop to message the carrier on their website and to find protocol for alerting them while traveling internationally. We wanted to let them know we did not need emergency services. We couldn't even turn the phone off. Later, we simply put it in a corner to let the battery drain and to maybe try it again later.

We went about our day continuing to enjoy our vacation. At the end of the day, the family one by one began to gravitate to their phones—all but my daughter whose phone was malfunctioning. We decided to have a no phone zone for the night and play more cards together. You may have seen those "No Phone Zone" signs around. We self-imposed a no-phone zone for the night! For the rest of us with working phones, it felt glorious. For her with a non-working phone, it felt debilitating.

It reminded us of a time when the kids were teenagers, and we had surprised them with a forced family fun trip! We rented an RV to do a family trip to Yellowstone, the Badlands, Grand Tetons and Mt. Rushmore. Scott and I pulled the RV up in front of the house and honked the horn. The kids came to the door, shaking their heads in disbelief! We said, "Leave your cell phones at the door! We are taking a family road trip!" Let's just say that trip had its challenges and didn't go quite as planned with three teenagers!

Nevertheless, here we were on this Christmas trip without a phone, unintentionally this time.

Day after day my daughter went without her phone. No photos, no internet searches, no email, and no Amazon surfing. At one point, she said, "All of my friends are going to think something has happened to me." Gone are the days where people memorize phone numbers of friends and family and can use someone else's phone to call someone! We later found out they did think something happened to her! Several were worried and had talked to their parents and let them know they couldn't reach her!

Per her request, we came home from the trip and went to the cell phone store the next business day. Unfortunately, it was a faulty screen with a hefty price tag to fix. We tried multiple options and other companies, but everyone was quoting hundreds of dollars. We got creative and pulled an old phone out of the junk drawer, which gave her a functioning phone, but there was still one problem. Her old phone had not backed up in well over a year, so she was worried about trying to restore the data even beyond fixing the device.

It was an "emergency" situation for her, and we could feel her tension and urgency as the days went on. Somehow her emergency became ours! She is set now, old working phone in hand.

As I have processed this after the fact, it made me examine myself. Do I get that alarmed when I do not have the Word of God at my fingertips? Do I feel as though other items and things are my lifeline outside of the Word of God? I'm sure I would feel my daughter's panic if that happened to my phone. But do I give that same care to my Bible?

What if a somewhat similar situation happened to you? What if your only Bible was a digital version on your phone? Would you be more distraught over losing photos, contacts, and internet access, or the Word of God?

The Message version of **Psalm 119:9-16** says,

> **How can a young person live a clean life? By carefully reading the map of Your Word. I'm single-minded in pursuit of You; don't let me miss the road signs You've posted. I've banked Your promises in the vault of my heart, so I won't sin myself bankrupt. Be blessed, God; train me in Your ways of wise living. I'll transfer to my lips all the counsel that comes from Your mouth; I delight far more in what You tell me about living than in gathering a pile of riches. I ponder every morsel of wisdom from You, I attentively watch how You've done it. I relish everything You've told me of life, I won't forget a word of it.**

Do you have a call you need to make to the Lord today? Don't wait until you are forced to operate in emergency mode. Some may be familiar with a "collect call," where the person receiving the call pays for the call! Christ already paid for your call! The debt has been paid. Take time to call upon the Lord. Talk to God about your concerns and shortcomings!

How can you make Monumental Moments and live to multiply His movement today?

DAY 89: GOD HAS A PLAN

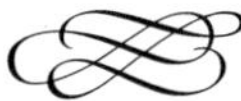

"Arise, go, and look," Kish said to his son Saul in **1 Samuel 9:13, NKJV**. Kish was sending his son on a journey to go and look for missing donkeys.

Though it was donkeys they were after, I'm sure it could have felt like a wild goose chase at the time.

Have you been in seasons or circumstances that have left you searching or feeling that all was lost? Have you grown tired or weary in the journey and wanted to simply turn around? Have there been times where it feels as though things just don't make sense?

Be encouraged! The King has a plan and is in control! He is going before you and orchestrating your steps. Though it may seem like you are aimlessly wandering, trust the Lord.

In **1 Samuel 9**, a troubling situation with missing donkeys from the family farm was used to send Saul on a mission searching for donkeys that eventually brought Saul before Samuel, the seer and man of God.

Saul obeyed his father's orders and went out into the hill country and passed through land after land looking for lost donkeys. Saul was gone for so long that at one point he turned to the young man with him and encouraged him that they should turn around and go back before his father began to be anxious about their whereabouts—worrying more about them than the donkeys.

Through it all, God went before Saul. The mission was bigger than chasing donkeys. The Lord spoke directly with Samuel ahead of time that a man from the land of Benjamin would arrive about this time tomorrow and he should anoint him as the prince over the people of Israel. A divine appointment was waiting for Saul.

In difficult situations, we can sometimes tend to see the chaos, confusion, and uncertainty and look at what is missing—especially if we do not see an end in sight. The Lord desires for us to keep Him at the forefront of every situation and search for Him in the midst of the journey. The King always knows the whole story!

We know that "**for those who love God all things work together for good, for those who are called according to His purpose,**" as we read in **Romans 8:28**.

Take a few moments today and read **1 Samuel 9**. May the Lord speak to you through His Living Word and help you to know He is going before you. What is He speaking to you through this story in the Bible?

There are divine appointments God has waiting for you! No matter what you are facing, may you trust the Lord has a beautiful plan with your name on it! He is orchestrating your steps. Be encouraged. He is worthy of your faithful pursuit! Arise warrior!

How can you make Monumental Moments and live to multiply His movement today?

DAY 90: EXITING AND ENTERING

Well, it's finally here . . . moving day and all the emotions that go with it. As if I didn't have enough boxes to move, I have truckloads of memories too. Memories of God's faithfulness; miracles; ministry; anniversaries; celebrations; birthdays; my children growing up; meals at the kitchen counter; conversations; disagreements; joblessness; breathtaking Colorado sunsets; stop-you-in-your-tracks sunrises; the kid's first days of school; scriptures written on the floors under the carpet; growth charts penciled on the pantry wall; cars driving away to college; hosting ministry leaders, loved ones, and even strangers; worship music echoing throughout the rooms; gut wrenching prayers prayed on my knees; and the sound of laughter, tears, and sometimes yelling. Through it all, it has been a peaceful sanctuary and retreat for our family and many others. It's God's home, and He has allowed my family the honor to stay here for the past 10 years.

It's the longest period we have stayed in one home. It was a home that answered so many prayers. It was a gift from God. We have come in and out of the front door a time or two, and today will be the last. I am overwhelmed with all the emotions as I reflect on God's blessings. Yes, the home is just stuff here on earth, but it is a place holding precious memories in my heart—thankfully ones I will continue to carry with me when I exit the door for the last time. It's time to follow God yet again, even when I don't have all the answers on what's next.

I heard a pastor once say, "The way you exit one door, determines the way you enter the next." So, how am I going to walk out of the door for the last time—sad, sorrowful, joyful, expectant, or thankful? I choose thankfulness in the midst of expectancy! A new season is here, and I will walk through it expectant and thankful.

Psalm 121:8 says, "**The Lord shall preserve your going out and your coming in from this time forth, and even forevermore.**" He will guard, watch over, protect, and preserve our going out and coming in. I love how the ESV version mentions going out first. We must take action. We must follow God. We must step out, and in doing so, the Lord will preserve us.

What is it that God is asking of you today? It may not be to sell a home in this season, but surely, He is asking something of you! Are you hesitant because you don't have all the details of what is next? Step out and watch God's faithfulness guard and protect you as you go out and come in! Trust Him. He always knows best! Reflect on His faithfulness with thanksgiving and trust and obey when He says, "Follow Me!"

How can you make Monumental Moments and live to multiply His movement today?

DAY 91: AND JUST LIKE THAT

Everyone loves a bonus! Our family gets the honor of having a bonus Dad. My father passed away quite some time ago after a very short and fierce battle with cancer. He will forever be loved and cherished in our hearts. We know He is living an eternal life with Christ Jesus, and we will one day see him again!

Years after Dad passed, Mom remarried to a wonderful man who loves the Lord, her, and our family so well. I call him Dad^2! He has a saying after our family gatherings and vacations, "And just like that: it's a wrap!" It's the exclamation mark to all our fun get-togethers. In some ways, as that statement wraps up one moment, it's almost creating a new charge in a sense—an encouragement that there's more ahead in the next!

Every time he says it, I feel such a sense of nostalgia as the memories of our time together flood my head. It's a precious gift I can carry with me.

We all have the opportunity to carry a precious gift with us in our journey! That's the eternal gift that God the Father gives us through His son Jesus Christ. We can walk with Him through every moment of life.

Psalm 91:1-16 says,

> **He who dwells in the shelter of the Most High will abide in the shadow of the Almighty. I will say to the Lord, "My refuge and my fortress, my God, in whom I trust." For He will deliver you from the snare of the fowler and from the deadly pestilence. He will cover you with His pinions, and under His wings you will find refuge; His faithfulness is a shield and buckler. You will not fear the terror of the night, nor the arrow that flies by day, nor the pestilence that stalks in darkness, nor the destruction that wastes at noonday. A thousand may fall at your side, ten thousand at your right hand, but it will not come near you. You will only look with your eyes and see the recompense of the wicked. Because you have made the Lord your dwelling place—the Most High, who is my refuge—no evil shall be allowed to befall you, no plague come near your tent. For He will command His angels concerning you to guard you in all your ways. On their hands they will bear you up, lest you strike your foot against a stone. You will tread on the lion and the adder; the young lion and the serpent you will trample underfoot. "Because he holds fast to Me in love, I will deliver him; I will protect him, because he knows My name. When he calls to Me, I will answer him; I will be with him in trouble; I will rescue him and honor him. With long life I will satisfy him and show him My salvation."**

When we choose to take refuge in the Lord and dwell in His presence from one moment to the next, He guards us in all our ways! When we call to Him, He will answer. He will show us His salvation.

What a gift to carry with us here on this earth and into eternity. For those that have surrendered their life to Christ and choose to live a life following God, you know how precious this gift of salvation is and the life-change that happens within your heart. Now we get the benefit of walking with our Father through all of life's moments—the hard, the heavy, and the heavenly together with God. How is your personal walk with Christ? How are you doing with helping introduce others to Jesus so they too can have their salvation moment?

I did not always understand the fullness of what Christ did for me through His death on the cross, nor understand the power of His resurrection. For years, I never even took time to ask why He would die for me. It's almost inconceivable. I spent the first 27 years of my life running from God and often did not even acknowledge there was a God. But then, just like that, there was a moment that changed everything. It was the moment I recognized Jesus as Lord and Savior —my Lord and Savior.

If you have not had your personal moment with God where you surrender your life to Him, may I encourage you to pause now and prepare for the greatest moment of your life? It will change you for eternity!

Romans 10:9-11 says,

> **Because, if you confess with your mouth that Jesus is Lord and believe in your heart that God raised Him from the dead, you will be saved. For with the heart one believes and is justified, and with the mouth one confesses and is saved. For the Scripture says, "Everyone who believes in Him will not be put to shame."**

John 14:6 says, **"Jesus said to him, 'I am the way, and the truth, and the life. No one comes to the Father except through Me.'"**

When you recognize Jesus as Lord, it will change the rest of your life and eternity. It did for me and has for billions of others!

If you want to choose to accept Jesus as your personal Savior, you can use the following prayer as your guide! It can be done anywhere, at any time. Don't delay. Your personal Monumental Moment with Jesus is here!

Prayer: Lord, I admit that I am a sinner in need of a Savior. I believe You sent Your one and only Son, Jesus Christ, to die for me and my sins. I believe You are the only way. I accept You as my Lord and Savior and choose to follow You all the days of my life, in Jesus' name. Amen!

If you prayed that prayer for the first time, congratulations and welcome to God's family! If you recommitted your life to Christ, welcome back home! And if you prayed that prayer and are living for Jesus already, great job! Keep passionately pursuing and proclaiming Jesus. We at Forge would love to help you activate the impact of your spiritual decision and empower your purpose!

Visit ForgeForward.org/next to connect with us today.

And just like that . . .

How can you make Monumental Moments and live to multiply His movement today?

ABOUT THE AUTHOR

Fun Fact: *Sparkle* is her favorite color!

Melissa is a devoted servant of the Lord with a life-changing story to tell! She lives to passionately pursue and proclaim Jesus and unashamedly shares the love of Christ and the Gospel message with people around the world—including in gas stations and bathrooms!

God wasn't a topic of conversation throughout Melissa's childhood. In fact, she didn't find Christ until the age of 27, when God stopped her in her tracks and changed everything as a new, stay-at-home mom. It was the greatest day of her life! She did a 180 and went from running from God to running to God and has been living with Him intimately ever after.

Melissa's heart beats to live in radical obedience and exhort others to do the same. After salvation, and a powerful transformation in her own life, she witnessed her husband, mother, father, sister, brother-in-law, sister-in-law, three children, father-in-law, friends, acquaintances, and even strangers surrender their lives to Christ, one by one.

She experienced the second and third greatest spiritual days of her life at the 2023 Asbury Revival when the Lord yet again set her heart ablaze with greater fire and intensity! As a gifted storyteller, communicator, and encourager, Melissa allows the Holy Spirit to use her everyday situations and life lessons to bring to life the transforming power of God's Word. Melissa is the host of the Monumental Moments podcast—a power-packed, 5-minute weekly devotional challenging Kingdom Laborers to live Monumental Moments to multiply His movement!

She has been married to her amazing husband, Scott, since 1996, and together they have three grown children. They share a passion for serving the Lord in their local church, community, around the world, and every place in between the Lord takes them. They work hard and play hard and love to explore new tropical destinations via boat at sea, underwater in scuba gear, and from sandy seashores—leaving footprints and fingerprints of Christ everywhere they go! Her family strives to live by the words spoken in **Joshua 24:15, "But as for me and my household, we will serve the Lord"** **(NIV)**.

facebook.com/melissa.motschenbacher
instagram.com/mmotsche

ACKNOWLEDGEMENTS

I am not the same person today that I was years ago (or even yesterday!) thanks to those that surround me and have challenged me to seek the Lord with everything I am. "Thank you" will never be enough. I am forever grateful for so many that have championed this monumental journey with the Lord!

§ The Lord Jesus Christ, the Savior of the World and of my soul.

§ Grandma Onlee, the precious one who prayed me into the Kingdom of God.

§ Lori Kolvek, the sweet friend who relentlessly invited me to a Bible study that introduced me to Jesus who changed everything.

§ Scott Motschenbacher, the amazing husband God set apart for me, and the man who sees my flaws and loves me through them all.

§ Kenzie, Peyton, and Kayla, my adored gifts from the Lord that continually teach me more of God's Heavenly perspective.

§ Carl Manis, my earthly father who taught me the fundamentals of generosity and helping others.

§ Connie and Chuck Brashers, my Mom and Dad^2 who are nothing but encouraging.

§ Monica Lee and family, my sister who is always up for a great conversation and processing the Word of God.

§ Christy Tiberg, my phone-a-friend lifeline and one of my biggest cheerleaders.

§ Emily Adams, a treasured friend, co-worker, and prayer partner that always points me to Jesus.

§ Motschenbachers, the loving family that welcomed me in with open arms as one of their own.

§ Forge Family, co-laborers leading me closer to Jesus daily; Dwight, Charlie, Santy, Board, Speakers, Firebrands, Operations Team, and Prayer Warriors.

§ Fellow Kingdom Laborers, so many of you have inspired me through the years to love the Lord with all my heart, soul, mind, and strength.

THANK YOU!

MORE FROM FORGE

FORGE SPEAKERS & EVENTS
ForgeSpeakers.org

Need someone to challenge your group to become passionate followers of Jesus who live with hearts on fire and lives on purpose? Book a Forge speaker for your next event!

FORGE EQUIPPING PROGRAMS for ALL AGES
ForgeTraining.org

Forge Equipping is not summer camp and training events "as usual." Forge challenges and equips people of all ages to become unique, lifelong Kingdom Laborers every day, everywhere.

FORGE BOOKS & RESOURCES
ForgeResources.org

Looking for a deeper relationship with God and practical ways to widen His Kingdom impact through your life? Forge has the resources you need.

THE FORGE APP

Essential Kingdom Laboring tools right at your fingertips:
TheForgeApp.org

JOIN THE MULTIPLYING MOVEMENT

Where everyday followers become Kingdom multipliers:
MultiplyingMovements.com

DEVOTIONAL CONTENT FOR THE EVERYDAY LABORER

Subscribe to the Monumental Moments podcast and devotionals:
MonumentalMoments.info

FORGE VIDEO CONTENT

Subscribe to free video content:
Youtube.com/ForgeForward

FORGE PODCAST

FuelForTheHarvest.com

FORGE DAILY TEXTS

Scan the QR code or visit ForgeForward.org/Sparks
to join Spark of the Day
for one-sentence daily devotionals.

NEED PRAYER?

Email us at Prayer@ForgeForward.org

CONTACT US

14485 E. Evans Avenue
Denver, Colorado 80014
303.745.8191
info@forgefoward.org

Learn more and get involved at
ForgeForward.org

Made in United States
Cleveland, OH
14 July 2025

18544181R00142